To friend Jane Sawyer
from Bob Abrams
2020

The Bare Bones Bible® Handbook

JIM GEORGE

HARVEST H
EUGENE, OREGON

All Scripture quotations are taken from the New King James Version. Copyright © 1982 by Thomas Nelson, Inc. Used by permission. All rights reserved.

Cover by Dugan Design Group, Bloomington, Minnesota

Cover photo © kevron 2001/Fotolia

Due to the intentionally brief treatment of each book of the Bible as presented in this handbook, disputed dates, themes, or authorships are not discussed. For such information, please consult more comprehensive reference works that are designed to take such various views and details into consideration.

THE BARE BONES BIBLE is a registered trademark of The Hawkins Children's LLC. Harvest House Publishers, Inc. is the exclusive licensee of the Federally registered trademark THE BARE BONES BIBLE.

THE BARE BONES BIBLE® HANDBOOK

Published 2014 by Harvest House Publishers
Eugene, Oregon 97402
www.harvesthousepublishers.com

ISBN 978-0-7369-5818-9 (pbk.)
ISBN 978-0-7369-5819-6 (eBook)

The Library of Congress has cataloged the edition as follows:

George, Jim 1943-
The bare bones Bible handbook / Jim George.
p. cm.
ISBN 978-0-7369-1654-7 (pbk.)
1. Bible–Introductions. 2. Bible—Handbooks, manuals, etc. I. Title.
BS475.3.G47 2006
220.6'1–dc22

2006013851

ISBN 978-0-7369-5818-9

Printed in the United States of America

18 19 20 21 / LB-CF / 11 10 9 8 7 6 5 4

Contents

Welcome to the Bible!

The Bible is unique among books. It declares itself to be written by God, the Creator of the universe. This all-powerful God used 40 inspired authors to pen the Scriptures over the course of 1500 years. The Bible is a written history of God's saving grace. From the very first chapter, God sovereignly moves history in a definite direction toward the consummation of all things in the new heavens and the new earth, where His name will be honored for all eternity and His voice obeyed by all the people of the earth.

Even though the Bible is an ancient book, its truths are as relevant today as when they were first written thousands of years ago. Because the Bible is God's revelation to mankind, its principles are timeless, giving answers to every question and need in your life.

It is my desire that the *Bare Bones Bible® Handbook* will become a tool to acquaint you with God's plan for the ages and enhance your present understanding of the Bible. I pray this handbook will stimulate you to a lifetime of discovering for yourself the amazing truths presented in God's Word, the Bible.

The Old Testament

The Historical Books

♁

The first 17 books of the Bible trace the history of man from creation through the inception and destruction of the nation of Israel. In the Pentateuch (the first five books of the Bible), Israel is chosen, redeemed, and prepared to enter a promised homeland. The remaining 12 historical books record the conquest of that land, a transition period in which judges ruled over the nation, the formation of the kingdom, and the division of that kingdom into northern (Israel) and southern (Judah) kingdoms, and finally the destruction and captivity of both kingdoms.

Genesis

In the beginning God
created the heavens and the earth.
(1:1)

♁

Theme: Beginnings
Date written: 1445–1405 B.C.
Author: Moses
Setting: Middle East

The Hebrew word for *Genesis* means "in the beginning," and that is exactly what Genesis is all about. As the first book of the Bible, Genesis lays out the foundations for everything that is to follow, including the key truths God wants you to know in order to make sense of your life. Throughout the pages of Genesis you experience the awesome power of God in His creation, the righteous judgment of God in the flood sent to punish the sinful disobedience of humanity, and the tender mercy of God in His protection of Noah and his family from the flood. You also witness the wondrous grace of God as He sets in motion His plan to redeem humanity, first through the founding of the nation of Israel, and ultimately through the sending of Jesus Christ. Genesis is filled with key moments that form the very basis of history.

The Skeleton

▸ **Chapters 1–2** *The Creation*

God creates the earth out of nothing, a perfect habitation for Adam and Eve, the first man and woman. He places them in the idyllic Garden of Eden and blesses their relationship.

▸ **Chapters 3–5** *The Fall and Its Aftermath*

The perfection of God's creation is disrupted when Satan tempts Adam and Eve to disobey God and usurp His rule over their lives, trying to become like gods themselves. When they give in to this temptation—referred to as "the fall"— they damage their relationship with God, are driven from the Garden, and must live outside the original blessing God intended for them. (However, even in the midst of this calamity, God is already setting in motion His long-term plan to redeem humanity and bring man back into an intimate relationship with Him.) Following the sin of their original parents, the human race degenerates into violence, wickedness, and self-destruction.

▸ **Chapters 6–11** *The Flood and a New Beginning*

In His displeasure with the wickedness of humanity, God determines to destroy man with a worldwide flood. Only Noah (a righteous man) and his family are spared from the devastation. From Noah's family the earth is repopulated as they spread out and form the first nations.

▸ **Chapters 12–25** *The Story of Abraham*

God calls Abraham to leave his home country and travel to a promised land, and tells Abraham he will become the father of His chosen people. To Abraham God gives many promises, one of which is that he—a childless old man—will have many descendants who will form a great nation, a people through whom salvation will come. This promise would be fulfilled in Abraham's greatest descendant, Jesus Christ.

▸ **Chapters 24–28** *The Story of Isaac*

Growing old and still without a child, Abraham begins to despair. But true to God's promise, Isaac is born to Abraham and his wife Sarah in their old age.

▸ **Chapters 28–36** *The Story of Jacob*

Isaac has two sons, Jacob and Esau. Although Isaac favors Esau, the eldest brother, Jacob schemes to secure the privileges of the birthright from his father. In fear of Esau's anger at being swindled out of his birthright, Jacob is forced to flee for his life. After many adventures, including a mysterious late-night wrestling match with God, Jacob finally matures into the man God intends him to be. God renames him *Israel,* which means "He who struggles with God," and Jacob's 12 sons become the 12 tribes of Israel.

▸ **Chapters 37–50** *The Story of Joseph*

Genesis closes with the account of Joseph, the favored son of Jacob, who is tragically sold into slavery into Egypt by his jealous brothers. But God has plans for Joseph and triumphantly establishes him as a leader in Egypt, which makes it possible for Joseph's family to later settle there with him and survive a devastating seven-year-long famine.

Putting Meat on the Bones

In addition to the great events such as the creation of the universe, the fall, the flood, and the founding of Israel, God also wants readers to become acquainted with the individual people who will be a part of His plan for redeeming the human race. The people He chooses are not perfect saints. They are, at times, deeply flawed in character and action. Genesis records that they lie, deceive others, question God, or are excessively proud—but God is able to use them anyway. This is one of the wonderful messages of the book of Genesis: The God who created us is not finished with us. He is in the business of "re-creating" us, giving us new beginnings and helping us become the kind of people He desires us to be.

Fleshing It Out in Your Life

Just as with Abraham, Jacob, Joseph, and others in Genesis, God can do great things through weak vessels, including you. By His grace and because of His sovereign plan, your mistakes and shortcomings do not disqualify you from being part of His grand plan, a plan still being worked out in you!

Life Lessons from Genesis

- God, the unique and sovereign Creator, made you and knows you better than you know yourself.

- God created you in His image, as an expression of Himself.
- God uses people with feet of clay—the imperfect, the failures, the flawed—to accomplish His will.
- God takes evil seriously, and those who reject His love and wisdom will experience His judgment.
- God is well able to turn your tragedies into triumphs.

Where to Find It

The story of creation . . . . Genesis 1:1–2:3
The first prophecy about Jesus . . . . Genesis 3:15
The account of Noah and the ark . . . . Genesis 6:1–8:22
Abraham told to sacrifice his son Isaac . . . . .Genesis 22:1-14
Jacob dreams of the ladder to heaven . . . . .Genesis 28:10-22
Jacob wrestles with God . . . . .Genesis 32:22-32
Joseph interprets Pharaoh's dreams . . . . .Genesis 41:1-36

Bare Bones Facts about Abraham

- He was a descendant of Shem, one of Noah's sons.
- He married his half-sister, Sarah.
- He courageously rescued his nephew Lot by defeating a powerful foe.
- His name was changed by God from *Abram* to *Abraham,* meaning "father of multitudes."
- He was known as a friend of God (2 Chronicles 20:7).
- His many acts of obedience and trust testified to his faith in God.
- He was the father of the Jewish and Arabic nations.
- He lived 175 years.

Exodus

I have come down to deliver them out
of the hand of the Egyptians,
and to bring them up from that land
to a good and large land....
(3:8)

♁

Theme: Deliverance
Date written:1445–1405 B.C.
Author: Moses
Setting: From Egypt to Mount Sinai

The time that passes between the final verse of Genesis and the first verse of the book of Exodus is about 400 years. During those four centuries, the 70 members of Jacob's family (who settled with Joseph in Egypt in order to survive a severe famine) multiply to over two million. New kings who do not know of Joseph and his vital role in making Egypt's survival possible are ruling the land. Out of fear of this growing population of Israelites, these new kings force the children of Israel to become slaves. Exodus is a record of God delivering His people from bondage and leading them to Mount Sinai to receive instructions on how to worship and serve Him as God.

The Skeleton

▸ **Chapters 1–6** *Bondage*

When the suffering Israelites cry out to God for deliverance, God responds by giving them an advocate. This man, named Moses, has been uniquely prepared for this task by God. He was born a Hebrew slave, adopted by the Pharaoh's daughter, and educated in the house of the king. He failed at an attempt to take a role of leadership over the Israelites, and spent 40 years as a shepherd in the desert. At last Moses is ready for leadership and, at a burning bush, receives his call to lead the nation of Israel. After some reluctance and many excuses, Moses obeys God, approaches Pharaoh, and requests that the Israelites be allowed to leave Egypt.

▸ **Chapters 7–18** *Deliverance*

Pharaoh refuses Moses' request, so God shows Pharaoh ten dramatic and miraculous plagues to convince him to let the Israelites go. The final plague is the death of the firstborn male in every Egyptian family. The Angel of Death spares all the households of Israel because they followed God's instruction to sprinkle lambs' blood on their doorposts. Finally, Pharaoh releases the people, but he has an evil change of heart and pursues God's people. In one final confrontation with Pharaoh, God displays His power as the Egyptian army and Pharaoh are drowned in the Red Sea. With great rejoicing, the Israelites travel on to Mount Sinai to receive their instructions for worshipping and serving God.

▸ **Chapters 19–31** *Instructions at Sinai*

Upon reaching Sinai, Moses goes up the mountain to receive the Ten Commandments, God's rules for His people to live by. While Moses is on the mountain, God also gives him many social and religious regulations for everyday living. In addition, Moses is given the details for the construction of God's tabernacle for worship.

▸ **Chapters 32–34** *God's Commitment Tested*

While Moses is on the mountain receiving God's instructions for holy living, the people below are committing sins of the worst kind—idolatry and immorality. God, in holy, righteous anger, desires to destroy the people and start over again with Moses. But Moses intercedes, appealing to God's character and mercy. As a result, the fellowship between Israel and God is renewed and the people recommit themselves to obeying God.

▸ **Chapters 35–40** *Building the Tabernacle*

After repenting for worshipping a golden calf, the people of Israel willingly give their possessions to build a tabernacle and its furnishings, and to sew garments for the high priest. The book of Exodus ends with the completion of the tabernacle and God coming to dwell in the tent and filling it with all His glory.

Putting Meat on the Bones

Having been slaves for 400 years, it is difficult for the Israelites to adjust to freedom. Slavery in Egypt had its benefits, as Egypt was the center of the world at that time. All the wealth and learning of the world funneled its way to Egypt. Even though the Israelites were harshly handled, they did have food and shelter. After they are delivered from Egyptian bondage, the children of Israel often look back on their days of slavery with lustful longing, forgetting that they were treated inhumanely.

Fleshing It Out in Your Life

As He did with the Israelites, God extends deliverance to you from slavery—slavery to sin—through the shed blood of God's perfect lamb, the Lord Jesus Christ. But, like the Israelites, you are often tempted to look back, longing for the pleasures of sin while forgetting the harsh cruelty of living under sin's bondage. Let Exodus remind you of your deliverance. Keep looking forward! Keep remembering the glory of God and His Son's victory over your sin.

Life Lessons from Exodus

- God hears the cries of His people and delivers them.
- Preparation for spiritual leadership takes time.
- When God selects you for a task, no excuses are acceptable.
- God demands your wholehearted, undivided worship.
- Praying for others is a vital element in your Christian life.
- Repentance restores your fellowship with God.

Where to Find It

The burning bush . . . . Exodus 3:1-12
The ten plagues . . . . Exodus 7:14–12:33
The death of Pharaoh and his army . . . . Exodus 14:15-28
The provision of manna . . . . Exodus 16
The principle of delegation . . . . Exodus 18:1-27
The Ten Commandments . . . . Exodus 20:1-17
The worship of the golden calf . . . . Exodus 32:1-35

The Ten Plagues

1. Blood (7:20)
2. Frogs (8:6)
3. Lice (8:17)
4. Flies (8:24)
5. Diseased cattle (9:6)
6. Boils (9:10)
7. Hail (9:23)
8. Locusts (10:13)
9. Darkness (10:22)
10. Death of the firstborn (12:29)

Leviticus

For I am the L*ORD* *your God....*
you shall be holy; for I am holy.
(11:44)

Theme: Instruction
Date written: 1445–1405 B.C.
Author: Moses
Setting: Mount Sinai

By the time the book of Exodus ends, one year has gone by since God's people left Egypt. During that year, two new developments have taken place in God's dealings with His people. First, God's glory is now residing among the Israelites; and second, a central place of worship—the tabernacle—now exists. As Leviticus opens, the Israelites are still camping at the base of Mount Sinai in the wilderness.

However, there are several elements of worship still missing, and Leviticus contains the instructions for these. A structured and regulated set of sacrifices and feasts are to be observed. Also a high priest, a formal priesthood, and a group of tabernacle workers must be appointed. In Exodus 19:6, God calls Israel to be "a kingdom of priests and a holy nation." Leviticus is filled with God's instructions on how His newly redeemed people are to worship.

The Skeleton

▸ **Chapters 1–7** *The Laws of Acceptable Worship*

Leviticus opens with God calling to Moses from the tabernacle. God tells Moses to instruct the people on how to have personal access to God through the offering of five different types of sacrifices. Then God gives Moses instructions for the priests on how they are to assist the people with each of these five sacrifices.

▸ **Chapters 8–10** *The Laws Pertaining to the Priesthood*

Up to this point in man's worship, people such as Abraham, Job, and other godly individuals have offered personal sacrifices to God. But now Aaron (the high priest and Moses' brother) and his sons and their descendants are ordained by God to take on the role of those who will offer the sacrifices for the people.

▸ **Chapters 11–16** *The Laws for Uncleanness*

In this section God uses everyday issues of life (such as food, animals, childbirth, disease, clothes, and bodily functions) to impress upon the people the differences between what is holy—or "clean"—and what is unholy—or "unclean." God gives no explanations or reasons for His instructions. He merely states that these are His standards and that the people are to obey them.

▸ **Chapters 17–27** *The Laws of Acceptable Living*

Moses continues to emphasize personal holiness to the people as their proper response to the holiness of God. Moses gives details on how the Israelites could make themselves spiritually acceptable to God. He also warns them about the consumption of blood, proper sexual practices, honoring their parents, and other issues related to holy living.

Putting Meat on the Bones

Throughout the book of Leviticus there is continual instruction regarding dedication to personal holiness in response to the holiness of God. This emphasis is repeated over 50 times through the phrases "I am the Lord" and "I am holy." Israel had very little knowledge of how to worship and live for God. They had lived in a land filled with many pagan gods and their sense of morality was sadly distorted, as witnessed by their "golden calf experience." God could not permit the Israelites to continue to worship in a pagan way or to live with pagan values. With the instructions in Leviticus, the priesthood would lead the people in acceptable worship and godly living.

Fleshing It Out in Your Life

Whether you realize it or not, your perspectives are being challenged or distorted by the pagan culture around you. Your worship and morality are constantly being influenced—or informed, fashioned, molded (Romans 12:2)—by an ungodly society. But God gives you His instruction book, the Bible, to correct any warped values and teach you how to properly live and worship in a way that is acceptable to Him. Be careful not to disregard God's instructions. Read His instructions in your Bible to understand what a holy God demands for holy living.

Life Lessons from Leviticus

- God is holy and demands holy living from His people.
- God states there are acceptable and unacceptable ways to worship Him.
- God has exacting standards for living.
- God says obedience to His standards results in blessing, while disobedience is punished.

Where to Find It

The beginnings of the priesthood . . . . Leviticus 8:1-36
The ordination of Aaron as high priest . . . . Leviticus 8:1-36
The sin of Nadab and Abihu . . . . Leviticus 10:1-7
The religious festivals of Israel . . . . Leviticus 23

The Life of Moses

- Called the greatest of all Old Testament prophets
- Authored the first five books of the Bible
- Was a prince of Egypt
- Had a sister and brother, Miriam and Aaron
- Was educated in all the knowledge of Egypt
- Was trained in desert survival as a shepherd
- Knew God face to face
- Lived 120 years
- Received the Ten Commandments twice

The Location of Mount Sinai

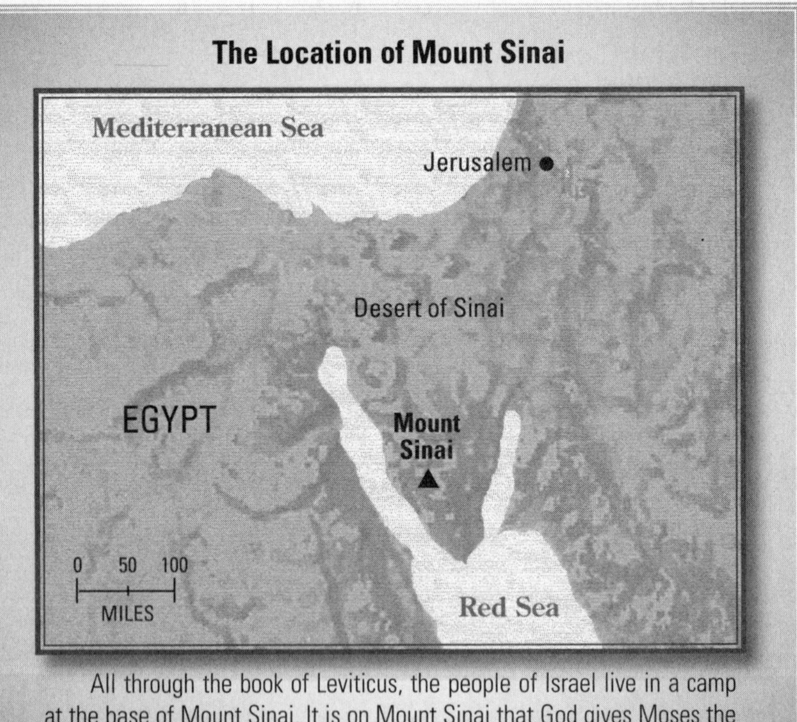

All through the book of Leviticus, the people of Israel live in a camp at the base of Mount Sinai. It is on Mount Sinai that God gives Moses the Ten Commandments and other instructions for right living.

Numbers

These are the journeys of the children of Israel,
who went out of the land of Egypt by their
armies under the hand of Moses and Aaron.
(33:1)

Theme: Journeys
Date written: 1445–1405 B.C.
Author: Moses
Setting: The wilderness

The book of Numbers is written in the final year of Moses' life, and concentrates on events that take place in the second and fortieth years after he led the nation of Israel out of Egypt to freedom. Everything recorded in Numbers 1–14 occurs in the year after the exodus, and the events of the Israelites' 38 years of wilderness wanderings are condensed into Numbers 15–19. Chapters 20–36 chronicle the fortieth year after the deliverance of God's people. This journey of 39 years from Mount Sinai to the plain of Moab records the experiences of *two generations* of the nation of Israel.

The Skeleton

▸ **Chapters 1–14** *The Old Generation*

The first generation of the nation of Israel participated in the exodus from Egypt. The details of their story begins in Exodus 2:23, when they were slaves in Egypt, and continues through the book of Leviticus and into the first 14 chapters of Numbers. This generation is "numbered" as a census is taken of the active warriors for the conquest in Canaan, the

Promised Land. They are given special instructions before they depart to journey from Sinai to Canaan. They then march, along with their families, to the borders of the Promised Land. However, when this generation of warriors arrives at the edge of their new home, they refuse to enter the land because of a terrifying report from ten of the 12 men sent forth to spy out the land. Because of this rebellion against the Lord's command, all the adults 20 years of age and older are sentenced to die in the wilderness. Only Caleb and Joshua, the two spies who gave affirming reports that the land should be taken, will live to enter the new land.

▸ **Chapters 15–20** *The Tragic Transition*

In these chapters, the ***first and second generations*** overlap. The first dies out as the second generation grows to adulthood. These chapters provide a sad ending to what begins with such promise. In chapter 20, Moses becomes angry with the continual murmuring of the people. He then disobeys God's command on how he was to provide water for the people. As judgment, God decrees that Moses will not lead Israel into the land of Canaan. A final act of transition from the first to second generations comes with the death of Aaron, Moses' brother and God's high priest.

▸ **Chapters 21–36** *The New Generation*

Like the first generation, ***the second generation*** journeys to the borders of the land. They too are given instructions, and again a census is taken before the invasion of the Promised Land. Moses appoints Joshua as his successor and the leader of this new generation. But, unlike the first generation, the second generation is not fearful of going to war, and within a short time will inherit the land.

Putting Meat on the Bones

In the first few verses of Numbers, God orders Moses to number the men aged 20 years and older who are able to go to war. (This initial selection is meant to help bring organization and discipline to this group of former slaves.) But before the Israelites go into battle, 12 spies are sent into the Promised Land to determine the strength of the enemy. Ten of the spies give a very negative report, saying God's people were "like grasshoppers" compared to the giants in the land. Even though God promised to give the Israelites the land, most of the spies did not believe the enemy could be conquered.

This negative report is contagious and the spies' unbelief is passed on to the entire army. They focus on the size of their enemy rather than on the size and greatness of their God. As judgment for their unbelief, God determines that all over the age of 20 must die in the wilderness. Only Joshua and Caleb are spared because their reports of the land focused on God's power and His promises. They believed God was able to give His people victory. God honored their belief and allowed them to finish their journey and enter the Promised Land.

Fleshing It Out in Your Life

What seemingly insurmountable problem are you facing today? What giant is causing you to cower? Learn a lesson from Joshua and Caleb and respond in faith. Focus positively on God's power rather than negatively on the problems at hand as you journey through life. Yes, the enemy is powerful, but God is more powerful! Declare boldly, "Through God we will do valiantly, for it is He who shall tread down our enemies" (Psalm 60:12).

Life Lessons from Numbers

- Order and discipline are essential for successfully completing your journey through life.
- Even when the odds are overwhelming, you can believe in God and His promises.
- Beware of the unbelief of others. It's contagious!
- Fearing others and failing to trust God has grievous consequences.
- Like Joshua and Caleb, don't follow the unbelief of the majority. Instead, have faith in God and reap the blessings.

Where to Find It

The report of the 12 spies . . . . .Numbers 13–14
The death of Miriam, Moses' sister . . . . Numbers 20:1
The death of Aaron . . . . Numbers 20:29
The bronze serpent . . . . .Numbers 21:4-8
The talking donkey of Balaam . . . . .Numbers 22:22-30
The appointment of Joshua as leader . . . . .Numbers 27:18-23

The Last Portion of Israel's Journey

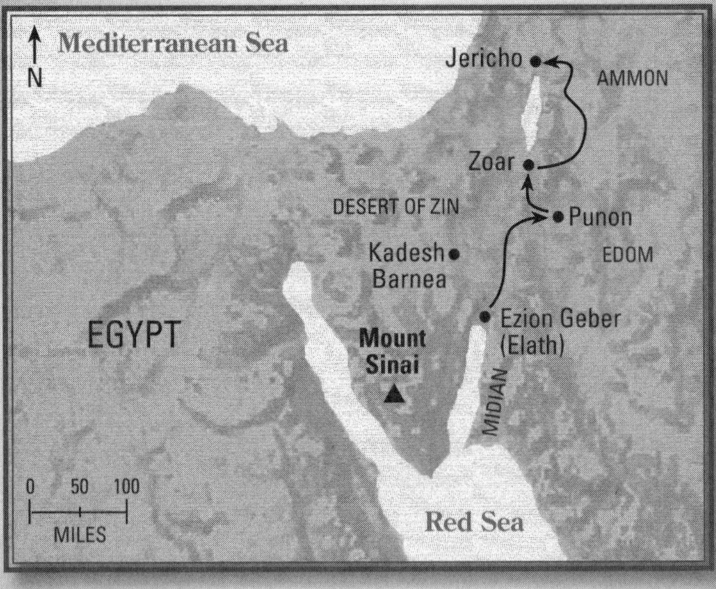

Israel spent 40 years in the wilderness. At the end of the people's journey, they camped on the east side of the Jordan River, ready to enter the Promised Land and to conquer the city-fortress of Jericho.

Deuteronomy

What does the L*ORD your God require of you,*
but to fear the L*ORD your God,*
to walk in all His ways....
(10:12)

Theme: Obedience
Date written: 1405 B.C.
Author: Moses
Setting: The plains of Moab

The book of Deuteronomy takes place entirely in one location over about a month of time. Israel is encamped east of the Jordan River across from the walled city of Jericho. It has been 40 years since the Israelites exited Egypt.

Deuteronomy concentrates on events that take place in the final weeks of Moses' life. The major event is the verbal communication of God's divine revelation that Moses had received over the past 39-plus years of wilderness wanderings. His audience is the new generation. They are poised and ready to enter the new land. This new generation needs this instruction in order to prepare for and prosper in their new land. The 120-year-old Moses gives three farewell speeches.

The Skeleton

▸ **Chapters 1–4** *The First Speech*

Looking back over time, Moses gives a historical review of the years and events from Mount Sinai to the present time as the children of Israel are camped on the plains of Moab.

▸ **Chapters 5–26** *The Second Speech*

Next, Moses reviews God's Ten Commandments and gives instructions about passing these commands on to succeeding generations. In addition, the ceremonial, civil, and social laws are reviewed for this new group of people before they inhabit the new land.

▸ **Chapters 27–30** *The Third Speech*

In dramatic fashion, as part of his final "sermon," Moses positions half the people on one mountain, and half on an opposite mountain. He then has the nation's leaders stand in the middle. Addressing first one side and then the other, Moses describes the immediate future with its blessings for obedience and curses for disobedience. He then prophesies what will happen in the distant future when Israel disobeys God, and in judgment, the people are scattered among the nations. Then Moses proclaims that, true to His promises, God will eventually bring the people back to their beloved land.

▸ **Chapters 31–34** *The Concluding Events*

In these closing chapters of the Pentateuch, the five books written by Moses, Joshua is again confirmed as the new leader of the Israelites. Moses then makes two more short speeches. The first is called "the song of Moses." In this prophetic song, Moses describes Israel's coming apostasy, God's judgment, and God's forgiveness and healing of both Israel and the land. In his second mini-speech, Moses gives his final blessing to each of the 12 tribes. Having fulfilled his role as a leader, Moses goes to the top of a nearby mountain, Nebo, and looks out over the Promised Land on the other side of the Jordan River. Then he dies, and is buried by God.

Putting Meat on the Bones

The book of Deuteronomy reveals much about the character and nature of God. How privileged the world is to have this written testimony of God and His dealings with His people! Any time we forget about some aspect of God's character or His work in history, we can simply pick up the Bible and read Deuteronomy.

But this was not the case in Moses' day. The only way to remind this new generation of the wonderful character of God was to rehearse it with them, to orally review for them how God honors obedience to His commandments and punishes disobedience. Moses also recounts the people's past history of rebellion and the consequences of their stubbornness. They are to learn a key lesson from the past: Disobedience brings consequences. But they are also to remember God is present with them, and if they dedicate their lives to Him and obey His laws, they will receive His blessings.

Fleshing It Out in Your Life

Moses' instructions concerning the character of God is still appropriate today. Learning about God will aid you in your love for Him and your pursuit of personal holiness. God is the standard. He is holy, and He expects holy behavior from His people. As a Christian, you are called to be holy as God is holy. You are to "love" Him "with all your heart, with all your soul, and with all your strength" (Deuteronomy 6:5).

Life Lessons from Deuteronomy

- Let your past failures prepare you for future victories.
- Realize God can blot out any sin, but He does not always take away its consequence.
- Never forget what you were saved from.
- Review God's Word regularly—it will guide your steps.

Where to Find It

The Ten Commandments reviewed . . . . Deuteronomy 5:7-22
"The Lord is one" . . . . .Deuteronomy 6:4
The command to love God . . . . Deuteronomy 6:4-9
The death of Moses . . . . .Deuteronomy 34:5

The Ten Commandments

1. Worship God alone (Exodus 20:3)
2. Do not worship images (Exodus 20:4)
3. Do not swear (Exodus 20:7)
4. Observe the Sabbath (Exodus 20:8)
5. Obey your parents (Exodus 20:12)
6. Do not murder (Exodus 20:13)
7. Do not commit adultery (Exodus 20:14)
8. Do not steal (Exodus 20:15)
9. Do not bear false witness (Exodus 20:16)
10. Do not covet (Exodus 20:17)

Joshua

As for me and my house,
we will serve the LORD*.*
(24:15)

Theme: Conquest
Date written: 1405–1385 B.C.
Author: Joshua
Setting: Canaan, the Promised Land

When Moses passed the baton of leadership on to Joshua (Deuteronomy 34), Israel was at the end of its 40 years of wilderness wanderings. Joshua had been Moses' faithful apprentice for most of that 40 years and was approaching 90 years of age when Moses calls him to become Israel's new leader. Joshua's task is to lead Israel into the land of Canaan, drive out the inhabitants, and divide the land among the 12 tribes.

The Skeleton

▸ **Chapters 1–5** *Preparation for Conquering the Land*

The book that bears Joshua's name opens with the people of Israel on the plains of Moab, east of the Jordan River, preparing spiritually, morally, and physically for the conquest of the land. Joshua and the Israelites are facing various peoples on the western side of the Jordan who make up a formidable and fierce enemy and live in heavily fortified cities. Yet God will give Israel the land by conquest, primarily to fulfill the covenant He pledged to Abraham and his descendants, but also to pass just judgment on the sinful inhabitants of the land because they had become so steeped in wickedness (see Genesis 15:16).

The conquest begins in a fashion similar to the exodus. The people must first cross a body of water. In this case it is the Jordan River, which is overflowing its usual banks because of the rainy season. As He did at the Red Sea, God holds back the waters of the Jordan River and the army of God passes through on dry ground.

▸ **Chapters 6–12** *Conquering the Land*

Now the army is poised and ready to begin the battle to gain their Promised Land. Israel's first test comes as the people are asked to let God provide the victory at the large and fortified city of Jericho. After the people walk around the city for seven days, God brings down its walls. This campaign in central Canaan drives a strategic wedge between the northern and southern cities, which prevents a massive alliance against Israel.

The southern and northern campaigns are also successful because Israel again allows God to fight for them. The only problem comes from a foolish oath made by the leaders of Israel to the deceptive Gibeonites, who pretended to be a people from a far-off country and asked for protection from Israel's armies. Because the Israelites fell for the ruse and gave an oath to protect the Gibeonites, Israel is forced to defend the Gibeonites and thus disobey God's command to eliminate all the Canaanites, including the Gibeonites.

▸ **Chapters 13–22** *Allocation of the Land*

Seven years later, after much of the conquest is completed, God tells Joshua to divide the land among the 12 tribes. The divisions are allotted, and the tribes are to continue the final conquests in their assigned areas.

▸ **Chapters 23–24** *Last Words of Joshua*

These closing chapters record Joshua's final challenge to the leaders to keep the law, and an exhortation to the people to serve the Lord.

Putting Meat on the Bones

The conquest of the land is to follow a simple "divide and conquer" strategy. Jericho is the key city in the central part of the land. God will use what sounds like a foolish military plan (walk around the city for seven days and then blow trumpets and shout on the last day). This command is a test to see if the people will recognize that a successful conquest must always come from God's power and not from their own abilities. And God's people passed the test with flying colors! They obeyed, blew their trumpets, and miraculously, the walls came tumbling down.

Fleshing It Out in Your Life

The book of Joshua teaches that when it comes to fighting the battles of life and gaining spiritual victory, blessing comes through obedience to God's commands. For you this means living your life by faith according to God's directions. Active faith does not require that you understand all or any of what God is doing in your life. You don't need to understand. You need only to obey and then reap the blessings of that obedience. God required the people to attempt the impossible, and it sounded like a crazy idea. Humanly speaking, walking around a fortified city and blowing trumpets should have no effect. But in God's realm, the impossible became possible and the people succeeded and gained the victory—God's victory. And just as God promised the Israelites victory, so has He also promised to give you victory. And like the Israelites, you must follow God's terms. Trust God. Attempt the impossible by submitting to God's directions, and watch the walls of your seemingly impossible problem miraculously come tumbling down.

Life Lessons from Joshua

- Faithfulness is a requirement for service.
- Serving others prepares you to lead others.
- Victory occurs when you let God fight your battles.
- Guidance from God for daily living comes from His Word, the Bible.
- At times you must make a stand for your beliefs.
- Living for God requires ongoing obedience.

Where to Find It

Rahab's protection of the spies .... Joshua 2:1-23
The conquest of Jericho .... Joshua 6:1–8:29
The sun stands still for a whole day ....Joshua 10:13
Caleb's request for land......................... Joshua 14:10-15
Joshua's stand for the Lord .... Joshua 24:14-15

Rahab's Place in Bible History

Rahab's courage...
was inspired by her faith in God's ability to deliver.
Rahab's faith...
made her one of only two women listed (Rahab and Sarah) in the Hall of Faith in Hebrews 11.
Rahab's descendants...
included David and later, Jesus.

Judges

When the children of Israel cried out to the LORD,
the LORD *raised up a deliverer….*
(3:9)

Theme: Deliverance
Date written: about 1043 B.C.
Author: Samuel
Setting: Canaan

Judges opens with the closing days of the life of the leader of God's people, Joshua, and gives a review of Joshua's death (see Joshua 24:28-31). Judges is a tragic sequel to the book of Joshua. In Joshua, the people were obedient to God and enjoyed victory in their conquest of the land. In Judges, however, they are disobedient, idolatrous, and often defeated and oppressed.

Like the earlier historical books, Judges presents historical facts, but in a very selective and thematic way. Foremost among its themes is God's power and covenant mercy in graciously delivering the Israelites from the consequences of their failures, which they suffered because of their sinful compromises (see 2:18-19; 21:25).

The book bears the fitting name *Judges,* which refers to 12 unique leaders God graciously raises up to deliver His people when they are oppressed as a result of their disobedience.

The Skeleton

▸ **Chapters 1–2** *The Military Failure of Israel*

The book of Judges opens with a short-lived military success after

Joshua's death. Israel's success quickly turns to repeated failures by all the tribes in their attempts to drive out their enemies. Instead of removing the godless inhabitants of the land, the tribes compromise spiritually. Therefore, God announces judgment and allows the godless nations to remain in the land as a test of Israel.

▸ **Chapters 3–16** *The Rescue of Israel by the Judges*

The people of Israel go through a series of cycles that contain a four-part sequence:

1. Israel departs from God.
2. God chastises Israel by permitting military defeat and oppression.
3. Israel prays for deliverance.
4. God raises up judges, either civil or military champions, who lead in the defeat of the oppressors.

Afterward, the people fall back into idolatry, which repeats the cycle.

▸ **Chapters 17–21** *The Moral Failure of Israel*

The content in this section actually precedes much of the information from chapters 3–16, but because of the book of Judges' thematic approach, the author wants to end with two bizarre illustrations, one showing religious apostasy (17–18) and the other describing social and moral depravity (19–21). The last verse of Judges (21:25) gives the key to understanding this period in the history of Israel: "In those days there was no king in Israel; everyone did what was right in his own eyes."

Putting Meat on the Bones

The book of Judges describes seven cycles of Israel's drifting away from the Lord, beginning even before Joshua's death, with a full departure into apostasy afterward. These cycles of apostasy and deliverance cover the whole land, as witnessed by the fact that each area of the land is specifically identified:

southern (3:7-31)
northern (4:1–5:31)
central (6:1–10:5)
eastern (10:6–12:15)
western (13:1–16:31)

Even with the widespread idolatry, immorality, and violence in Israel, God was ever faithful to deliver the people. In His gracious love for His people, God continued to forgive them every time they cried out to Him.

Fleshing It Out in Your Life

How often can it be said of you that you "do what is right in your own eyes"? It's easy to act in foolishness, ingratitude, stubbornness, and rebellion and then wonder why you live in such utter defeat and suffering. The God of Judges is the same God of today. And as then, when you cry out to God in repentance, He is nearby to faithfully forgive and deliver you. Are you living in spiritual defeat? Cry out to God. He is ready to send deliverance!

Life Lessons from Judges

- Don't compromise with the world—it leads to defeat.
- Don't sin—it results in suffering.
- Don't wait until you are without hope to cry out to God.
- Don't do what is right in your own eyes—do what's right in God's eyes.

Where to Find It

Deborah, the only female judge . . . . Judges 4–5
Gideon and his 300 men . . . . Judges 7:1-7
Samson and Delilah . . . . Judges 16:4-22
Israel and the war against the tribe of Benjamin Judges 20

The Judges *versus*	**Their Enemies**
Othniel	The Mesopotamians
Ehud	The Moabites and Ammonites
Shamgar	The Philistines
Deborah	The Canaanites
Gideon	The Midianites
Tola and Jair	The evil of Abimelech
Jephthah, Ibzan, Elon, Abdon	The Ammonites
Samson	The Philistines

Samson's Life

- Dedicated as a Nazarite to God
- Parents talked to God twice
- Used his great strength to free Israel
- Was controlled by sensuality
- Violated his vows on many occasions
- Used his abilities for selfish purposes
- Put his confidence in the wrong people
- Used by God in spite of his mistakes
- Listed in God's Hall of Faith in Hebrews 11

Ruth

Your people shall be my people,
and your God, my God.
(1:16)

Theme: Redemption
Date written: 1030–1010 B.C.
Author: Unknown/possibly Samuel
Setting: Moab and Bethlehem

The book of Ruth takes place during the spiritually dark days of the Judges. Ruth is the story of a woman (named Ruth) who lives during this evil period in Israel's history but does not succumb to its moral decay. Ruth's story is one of integrity, righteousness, and faithfulness. Her story covers about 11–12 years. She and Esther are the only women who have books of the Bible named after them.

The Skeleton

▸ Chapter 1 *Ruth's Faithfulness*

Ruth's story opens with a severe famine in the land of Israel, including the town of Bethlehem. This famine forces an Israelite named Elimelech to move his wife, Naomi, and their two sons to Moab, a country to the east. While living there, both sons marry Moabite women but subsequently die, as does their father. Now left alone, Naomi decides to return to her homeland and suggests that her two daughters-in-law, Ruth and Orpah, remain in their own land with their people and kin. Orpah chooses to stay and is never heard of again. Ruth, however, chooses to cling to

Naomi and follow the God of Israel. Because of her desire to be faithful to Naomi, Ruth gives up her gods, her culture, and her people.

▸ **Chapter 2** *Ruth's Service*

Naomi returns to Bethlehem a bitter woman, thinking God is her enemy because of her losses. But God has plans she doesn't know about, which begin to unfold when Ruth volunteers to go into the fields around Bethlehem to pick up the grain left behind by the harvesters. Such gleaning was permitted to provide for the poor of the land. In God's plan and providence, Ruth enters the field of a man named Boaz, a relative of Naomi's. Boaz has heard of Ruth's faithfulness toward his relative Naomi and gives instructions to his workers to leave grain behind and thus provides for her and Naomi.

▸ **Chapter 3** *Ruth's Proposal*

Over a period of several months and through the different harvests, Ruth willingly works in Boaz's fields to provide for her and Naomi. But now it is time for Naomi to repay Ruth's kindness and provide for Ruth's future. She devises a plan that will force Boaz to make a more serious decision about Ruth. Ruth is instructed by Naomi to engage in a common, ancient Near-Eastern custom of asking Boaz to take her for his wife in the place of her dead husband because he is a close relative (see the levirate marriage principle of Deuteronomy 25:5-6). All of this takes place at night on a threshing floor during the harvest.

Ruth's proposal is accepted when Boaz throws a garment over her. (This symbolic action also appears in Ezekiel 16:8, where Jehovah spreads His garment over Israel.) Even though Ruth sleeps at Boaz's feet through the night, there is no hint of improper behavior.

▸ **Chapter 4** *Ruth's Reward*

Boaz agrees to marry Ruth as a close relative, but reveals the next morning that he must first ask another man, a closer relative, to see if that man wanted to fulfill the levirate custom. In this final chapter we see Boaz come before the local elders and, with them as witnesses, ask the closer relative about Ruth. The man declines, thus permitting Boaz to marry Ruth. God blesses Ruth's faithful devotion by giving her a husband in Boaz and a son, Obed, who would later be the grandfather of the famous future king of Israel, David.

Putting Meat on the Bones

The book of Ruth gives great encouragement as God provides an example of godly behavior in the midst of widespread ungodliness during the time of the Judges. Ruth's faithfulness to follow the God of Israel leads to great blessing not only for her, but for Naomi, for Boaz, and ultimately for the world as she takes her place in the family line of Jesus Christ.

Fleshing It Out in Your Life

In addition to seeing Ruth's faithfulness to the God of Israel and to Naomi, we also see Boaz's integrity and faithfulness in action. Boaz became a kinsman-redeemer, or a close relative who in essence redeems the Gentile Ruth and gives her a home. Their union produces a son, whose grandson is David, and whose ultimate ancestor is Jesus Christ. The book of Ruth gives us an important analogy of the work of Christ. Like Boaz, Jesus is related to us by His physical birth, able to pay the price of redemption, willing to redeem, and able to redeem. And like Ruth, you must choose to accept redemption and leave the transaction to Jesus, who makes the redemption a reality. Don't be like Ruth's sister-in-law, who chose to return to her pagan gods and was lost forever. Come to Jesus—who is your Kinsman-Redeemer—and live forever.

Life Lessons from Ruth

- What you think to be a tragedy is God's opportunity to show Himself faithful.
- Your abundance is an opportunity to help the less fortunate.
- God honors faithfulness.
- Character is a noble quality that God honors.
- Adverse circumstances give you the opportunity to exhibit godly character.

Where to Find It

Ruth's loyalty to Naomi .... Ruth 1
Boaz's kindness to Ruth .... Ruth 2
God's provision of a kinsman-redeemer .... Ruth 3
Christ's lineage through Ruth .... Ruth 4

Boaz
Portrait of a Godly Man

Diligent	Ruth 2:1	Generous	Ruth 2:15
Friendly	Ruth 2:4,8	Kind	Ruth 2:20
Merciful	Ruth 2:7	Discreet	Ruth 3:14
Godly	Ruth 2:12	Faithful	Ruth 4:1-9
Encouraging	Ruth 2:12; 3:11		

1 Samuel

Behold, to obey is better than sacrifice….
(15:22)

♁

Theme: Transition
Date written: 930–722 B.C.
Author: Unknown
Setting: The struggling nation of Israel

The book that precedes 1 Samuel—Ruth—is indeed, a bright spot in a dark land and a love story with many happy endings. We now arrive at a transition in the history of God's people with three sets of "doubles"—

1 and 2 Samuel,
1 and 2 Kings, and
1 and 2 Chronicles.

There have been a multitude of books written about the history of great nations. Many of their titles start with the phrase *The Rise and Fall of*…. First and 2 Samuel, along with the other two "doubles," form their own history book, which we could entitle *The Rise and Fall of the Israelite Monarchy*.

Originally 1 and 2 Samuel were one book in the Hebrew Bible, but later translations separate them into our present two books. First Samuel is named for the first of three prominent personalities—Samuel, Saul, and David—interwoven throughout its contents.

The Skeleton

▸ Chapters 1–7 *Samuel*

Samuel's life story begins as the period of the Judges is coming to an end. Eli, the present judge-priest of Israel, has his residence at Shiloh, where the tabernacle is located. Samuel's mother Hannah is introduced as a barren woman who prays to God and vows that, if He would give her a son, she would dedicate him to the Lord for God's service all the days of his life. God responds to Hannah's prayer and gives her Samuel, who grew to faithfully judge Israel. When Samuel is old the people of Israel, wanting to be like the nations around them, naively cry out for a king. Sadly, one of the reasons they want a king is that Samuel's sons are unfit to judge in their father's place.

▸ Chapters 8–15 *Saul*

God gives the people their request and their first king, Saul, is anointed. Saul starts out well, but his good qualities begin to erode as he transitions into the pressures of being king and leading the people in battle. At an early point in Saul's reign, Samuel tells Saul to wait for Samuel's arrival to perform a ritual sacrifice. But in the midst of battle pressures, and because of his pride and impatience, Saul brashly assumes the role of a priest and offers up the sacrifice without waiting for Samuel. When Samuel shows up, he tells Saul, "You have done foolishly" (13:13).

Later Saul evokes a rash vow from his men regarding food just before they go into another battle. Then he disobeys God's command to destroy the Amalekites, whom he has just defeated. Finally and tragically, at the end of his 40-year reign, rejected by God and afraid of an impending battle against the Philistines, he foolishly consults a medium, or a witch, for counsel (see chapter 28). Saul's doom is pronounced, and he and his sons are killed the next day in battle.

▸ Chapters 16–31 *David*

Recall again that the lives of Samuel, Saul, and David are threaded throughout this book. Although Saul is still reigning, there is no mistaking that the main focus of the book is now shifting to David. His story begins as Saul is rejected by God for his disobedience. Samuel is commissioned to anoint David, Israel's next king. God's presence with David thrusts him into prominence as David kills the Philistine giant

Goliath, fights many successful battles, and becomes a devoted friend to Jonathan, Saul's eldest son.

David becomes a growing threat to the obsessively jealous Saul. He is initially protected by Jonathan, Michal (Saul's daughter and David's wife), and Samuel. But Saul becomes more active in his pursuit of David. Finally, David flees and ultimately ends up in a Philistine city, where he pretends to be insane in order to save his life. Then he flees again to a secret hideout, where a band of mighty men protect him. David continues to escape from the murderous hand of Saul and, on two occasions, spares Saul's life because he cannot bring himself to kill Israel's king even though Saul is trying to kill him. David continues to elude Saul until Saul and his sons are killed in a great battle with the Philistines.

Putting Meat on the Bones

Samuel provides a great illustration of how one man handled transition in his life. He was to be the last of the judges. Even though Samuel was a man of integrity all his life, the people rejected his offer for his sons to lead them and instead wanted a king so they could be more like the nations around them. Even with the rejection of his corrupt sons, Samuel steadfastly commits to praying for the people. In spite of the adverse changes that are happening to and around Samuel, he never falters in his faithfulness to God or God's people.

Now contrast Samuel's life with that of King Saul. Saul's transition from commoner to king is marked by pride, deceit, and a progressively unrepentant heart. He starts out well, but somewhere along the way, he decides not to follow God's commands, and chooses to chart his own course. Ultimately Saul's choice costs him his life and the lives of his sons, and places the nation of Israel in great peril.

Over the long haul, Samuel was able to make the adjustments necessary for his continued usefulness to both God and the people. Tragically, King Saul was not able to make the transition. Pride and arrogance were his downfall.

Fleshing It Out in Your Life

Transitions are a critical part of everyone's life. We move from one learned skill or developed ability to another, from one promotion to another. School gives way to work, and work gives way to retirement. We all pass from one season of life to the next. And ultimately, life shifts to death.

Whether you realize it or not, your life is in a constant state of change. Therefore you must recognize how crucial it is to make transitions well. And it's not the transition itself that's critical, but how you respond to the changes that come your way. Some people don't handle change well. They fall apart when faced with a new season in life. Or they can't handle new responsibilities or a lessening of responsibilities.

How do you make sure your life and attitudes honor God with each change that comes? Like Samuel, you want to stay faithful and close to God through prayer and the study of His Word. Then when a transition occurs, you will be prepared to draw on God's strength and honor Him with your godly attitudes and actions. And you will never skip a beat in your service to others.

Life Lessons from 1 Samuel

- A close walk with God will help you better handle life's transitions.
- Your faithful service will be rewarded, at least in God's eyes.
- God wants your inward commitment, not just an outward observance.
- It's not how you start that's important, but how you finish!

Where to Find It

Samuel's mother, Hannah .... 1 Samuel 1–2
Samuel's service to God as a child .... 1 Samuel 3
Saul is anointed as king .... 1 Samuel 10:1
David is anointed as king .... 1 Samuel 16:13
David's fight with the giant Goliath .... 1 Samuel 17
David's friendship with Jonathan .... 1 Samuel 18:1-4
Saul's visit with the witch of Endor .... 1 Samuel 28:7-19

Why Was Samuel the Most Influential Man of His Day?

- He was wholly devoted to God.
- He was wholly committed to God's people.
- He was wholly honest with the people.
- He was wholly compassionate concerning the people.

2 Samuel

Your house and your kingdom
shall be established forever....
(7:16)

Theme: Unification
Date written: 931–722 B.C.
Author: Unknown
Setting: United kingdom of Israel

Second Samuel picks up where 1 Samuel leaves off. Saul is now gone, so the people of Judah, David's ancestral tribe, declare David as their king, while the northern tribes acknowledge Saul's youngest son as their king. David rules in Hebron for seven-and-a-half years before all Israel finally acknowledges David as their king. He then reigns in Jerusalem for 33 years. Second Samuel reviews the key events in David's 40-year reign and, like 1 Samuel, the book can be divided into three main parts, with chapter 11 marking the turning point in the life and success of David.

The Skeleton

▸ Chapters 1–10 *David's Success*

Under David's leadership, the northern and southern tribes of Israel are united. David's success—both militarily and domestically—is remarkable. Under his leadership the nation shifts from tribal independence to a centralized government. He captures the city of Jerusalem and makes it his capital.

David, a man after God's own heart, shows mercy to Saul's family and rules with justice and fairness. He also brings the ark that was constructed at Mount Sinai to Jerusalem and desires to build a permanent temple to house the ark. God responds by reaffirming the covenant He originally made with Abraham, and assures David that one of David's descendants would always reign on his throne. This covenant is realized in David's distant son, the Lord Jesus Christ.

▸ **Chapter 11** *David's Sin*

David knows that the Lord is responsible for his success. He realizes that God wants to bless His chosen people, Israel. Yet, at the peak of his influence, David abandons his principles and commits adultery with a woman named Bathsheba. When she informs David that she is pregnant, David tries to cover up his sin and, in the process, engineers the death of Bathsheba's husband, Uriah, one of David's faithful soldiers. After a period of mourning, David takes Bathsheba as his wife and she bears him a son. Needless to say, God is displeased. From this point on David will experience continued struggles both within his family and with the nation.

▸ **Chapters 12–20** *David's Struggles*

God confronts David about his sin with Bathsheba and the murder of Uriah by sending the prophet Nathan. Nathan approaches David with a story about a man whose only lamb had been taken away by a man who had many lambs. David righteously condemns the latter man's action. At that point the prophet declares, "You are that man."

David confesses at last, but the consequence of his sin would be far-reaching and tragic. His son conceived with Bathsheba dies. His son Amnon commits incest with his half-sister Tamar. Absalom, Tamar's brother, kills Amnon and flees for his life. Later Absalom is allowed to return, but he soon schemes to overthrow his father David. Absalom almost succeeds, but is killed in a decisive battle. Civil war continues as a man named Sheba marshals the allegiance of the northern tribes, but he too is killed and further strife is averted.

▸ **Chapters 21–24** *David's Reflections*

These chapters categorically describe David's words and deeds. They show how ultimately, the moral and spiritual condition of the king affects the physical and spiritual state of the people. The nation of Israel enjoys God's blessings when David is obedient and suffers hardship when David disobeys God.

Putting Flesh on the Bones

In spite of his shortcomings, David remained a man after God's own heart. Why? Obviously it wasn't because David lived a sinless life. Far from that! He often failed in his personal life, but he never faltered in his desire for an ongoing relationship with God. David was God's man because of his responsive and faithful attitude toward God. After he had sinned, he realized his need to make things right with God through a repentant heart. Unfortunately, his repentance couldn't repair the damage brought about by his sin. Yes, he was forgiven. And yes, his relationship with God was restored. But the list of those who suffered from and because of David's sins is a long and tragic one.

Fleshing It Out in Your Life

Do you desire to be a man or woman after God's own heart? Realize that God isn't looking for perfection, for "all have sinned and fall short of the glory of God" (Romans 3:23). You, as God's man or woman, are not unblemished, but you are progressing. Hopefully you love God with all your heart and soul, and even though you stumble and fall at times, you are quick to ask God for forgiveness.

In David's life you see God's grace in action. He forgives His sinning children. You can thank God for His grace when you sin. But David's life also gives a sobering look at sin in action. You learn from David's suffering that sin is never committed in a vacuum. Others are always affected by our sin. Ask God for His strength to help you resist sin so that it doesn't affect your relationship with Him and bear consequences on others.

Life Lessons from 2 Samuel

- Blessing comes to you and those around you when you are obedient to God's commands.

- Conversely, there are always consequences to your sinful actions.
- Your role as a parent is a full-time job and must not be neglected or delegated to others.
- Repentance restores your relationship with God.

Where to Find it

The Davidic covenant . . . . 2 Samuel 7
David's sin with Bathsheba . . . . 2 Samuel 11
David's sin of numbering the people of Israel . . . . . . 2 Samuel 24:10-17

The Life of David

David was...

- An ancestor of Jesus Christ
- The killer of the giant Goliath when just a teenager
- The possessor of a repentant heart
- The cause for his family's suffering due to his sin
- The greatest king of Israel

1 Kings

Because you...have not kept
My covenant and My statutes...
I will surely tear the kingdom away from you….
(11:11)

Theme: Disruption
Date written: 561–538 B.C.
Author: Unknown
Setting: Israel

The story of 1 and 2 Kings is basically one of failure. The tiny nation of Israel had gained dominance in its region because God had blessed it. But at the height of their affluence and influence, the people plunged into poverty and paralysis as they turned away from God.

The Skeleton

▸ **Chapters 1–11** *Solomon and a United Kingdom*

The opening chapters describe the glorious reign of King David's son, Solomon. God had refused David's offer and desire to build Him a house and gave that privilege to Solomon instead. David's wars had cleared the way for Solomon, who erects the temple from materials David had prepared and gathered. The ark of the covenant is placed in the new temple, and the glory of the Lord fills the temple.

Solomon prays and asks God for wisdom and becomes the wisest and richest man alive. His many foreign wives, however, turn his heart away from God. God pronounces judgment and declares that Solomon's son would rule only a fraction of the kingdom.

▸ **Chapters 12–22** *The Kings and a Divided Kingdom*

After Solomon's death, Solomon's son Rehoboam antagonizes the ten northern tribes, which brings about a split in the kingdom. As predicted in a warning from God to Solomon, Rehoboam is left with two tribes, Judah and Benjamin. Jereboam, an officer in Solomon's army, leads a revolt and is made king of the northern tribes. This begins the chaotic period with two nations, two sets of kings, two religions, and two places of worship. The book of 1 Kings reports the reigns of both sets of kings in parallel fashion. Of all the kings, both northern and southern, only a few southern kings did what was right in the sight of the Lord. All the others were wicked idolaters and murderers.

The prophet Elijah ministers during the reign of Ahab, an exceptionally wicked northern king. Ahab's wife Jezebel introduces Baal worship to those in the northern kingdom. Elijah confronts Ahab and the prophets of Baal in a showdown on Mount Carmel, where God miraculously sends down fire and consumes a sacrifice well-doused with water by Elijah. Elijah goes on to kill the 450 prophets of Baal who were present at Mount Carmel.

Elijah then places his mantle on a younger man named Elisha, designating him as his understudy and successor. Elijah also continues to condemn Ahab for his wickedness until Ahab's death in battle.

Putting Meat on the Bones

Just before his death, David charged his son Solomon to "walk in [God's] ways, to keep His statutes, His commandments, His judgments, and His testimonies" (1 Kings 2:3). This Solomon did and, as you have already learned, when given a choice of riches, long life, or wisdom, Solomon humbly asked for wisdom. As a result, Solomon's reign began with great success. Unfortunately Solomon allowed his many pagan wives to turn his heart from following after God. Thus the wisest man on earth became a fool.

Rehoboam succeeded his father Solomon and had the opportunity to be a wise, compassionate, and just king. Instead, he accepted foolish advice from his young friends over the advice of his older and wiser counselors, which resulted in the split of the kingdom.

Fleshing It Out in Your Life

How ironic that the son of the wisest man on earth didn't or wouldn't take the advice of his father's many proverbs which speak of the importance of seeking, hearing, and heeding the advice of good counselors (Proverbs 11:14; 15:22; 24:6). Maybe Rehoboam observed the folly of his father's later life and wanted nothing to do with his father's wisdom from his earlier years. Whatever the reason, Rehoboam listened to his friends rather than to wise counselors—with disastrous consequences.

God has provided you with many avenues for obtaining wisdom for the variety and number of decisions you must make in your everyday life. Resist your human inclination to reject help and attempt to do things your own way. You have your Bible, the leading of the Holy Spirit, church leaders, and the wisdom of older men and women available to help in your decision-making process. Don't bypass these important resources, for they can help ensure that your decisions honor God and bless others.

Life Lessons from 1 Kings

- God has given you the stewardship of your life—use it wisely.
- Obedience to God will bring blessings to you and others.
- Wisdom is not a guarantee you won't act foolishly.
- Beware of worldliness—it can turn your heart from God.
- Don't let your personal desires distort the standards established in God's Word.
- Unless you serve God, you become a slave to whatever takes His place in your life.
- Pray unselfishly for that which will help others.

Where to Find It

Solomon's temple . . . . 1 Kings 5–8
Solomon's meeting with the Queen of Sheba . . . . 1 Kings 10
Jeroboam's golden calves . . . . 1 Kings 12:25-33
Elijah's encounter with the prophets of Baal . . . . 1 Kings 18
Elisha's call to follow Elijah . . . . 1 Kings 19:19-21

Miracles Performed by Elijah

Elijah's Miracles

- Multiplies a widow's food
- Raises a widow's son to life
- Calls down God's fire on an altar and its sacrifice
- Calls down fire on evil soldiers
- Parts the Jordan River

2 Kings

I will also remove Judah from My sight, as I have removed Israel, And will cast off this city Jerusalem....
(23:27)

Theme: Dispersion
Date written: 561–538 B.C.
Author: Unknown
Setting: Divided kingdoms of Israel and Judah

Second Kings continues without a break the history of the kingdoms of Israel and Judah. They both fling headlong toward a collision course with captivity as the glory of the once-united kingdom begins to fade into the distant past. When the end finally comes, with the northern tribes taken into Assyrian captivity and the southern tribes deported to Babylon, nine different dynasties are described for the northern kingdom, Israel. But, as promised to David, there is only one dynasty in Judah.

The Skeleton

▸ **Chapters 1–17** *The Divided Kingdoms*

These chapters record the continual downward spiral of both the northern and southern kingdoms. All the kings of the northern kingdom are recorded as evil and wicked. Even the miraculous ministries of Elijah and his successor, Elisha, have little effect. Of Israel's 19 kings, none did what was right in God's sight. Finally, God has enough and brings the Assyrian armies against Israel. They besiege Samaria, the capital, and overthrow the nation and deport the survivors back to Assyria.

Meanwhile, the situation in the southern kingdom of Judah is somewhat better but not ideal. Athaliah, the daughter of King Ahab and Jezebel of the north, follows in the wicked footsteps of her mother, killing all the descendants of David except for Joash. She then usurps the throne. Then according to God's promise to always have a descendant of David sitting on his throne, the priest, Jehoiada, eventually removes Athaliah and places the young lad, Joash, in power. Joash restores the temple and serves God.

▸ **Chapters 18–25** *The Surviving Kingdom*

The account of Judah, the surviving kingdom, reads more easily than the accounts of the divided kingdoms. There is no longer any alternating of the narrative between the two kingdoms. Only Judah is left. Six years before the overthrow of Samaria, Hezekiah becomes king of Judah. Because of Hezekiah's exemplary faith and reforms, God spares Jerusalem from Assyria and brings a measure of prosperity to Judah.

However, Hezekiah's son, Manasseh, is so wicked and his reign so long that Judah's downfall is imminent. Even Josiah's later reforms cannot stem the tide of evil, and the four kings who succeed Josiah are as wicked as Manasseh.

The book of 2 Kings ends with judgment coming in the form of three deportations into exile to Babylonia, the third occurring in 586 B.C. when Nebuchadnezzar destroys Jerusalem and the temple. Even with this destruction, the book ends on a note of hope as God preserves a remnant of people for Himself.

Putting Meat on the Bones

Even though 1 and 2 Kings are two separate books in today's Bibles, they were originally one and they share the same theme: When the kings follow God's covenant ways, they and their people prosper; but those kings who refuse to obey God are sure to face judgment. The decline and collapse of the two kingdoms occurs because of failure on the part of the rulers and the people to heed the warnings of God's prophetic messengers. God is seen in Kings as the controller of history, and the spiritual climate of the kingdoms determines their political and economic conditions. Because of disbelief and disobedience on the part of both the northern and southern kingdoms, God allows the Assyrians and Babylonians to take His people captive into exile.

Fleshing It Out in Your Life

Often on a national day of prayer, pastors will quote 2 Chronicles 7:14: "If My people who are called by My name will humble themselves, and pray and seek My face, and turn from their wicked ways, then I will hear from heaven, and will forgive their sin and heal their land." While this scripture is a call for Israel to repent and return to her godly heritage, it can serve as a calling to you as well. Like Israel, you provide a sobering example to others of the necessity of obeying God.

Instead of adopting the ways of the godless, turn from them and humbly call upon God. Nurture a heart of contrition. Willingly humble yourself and pray and seek God's face and turn from any practices that are displeasing to the Lord. This is the path to forgiveness and blessing!

Life Lessons from 2 Kings

- God is patient. He gives you many opportunities to heed His call to repentance and obedience.
- Even when others around you are disobedient, you are to be obedient, for you are responsible for your own actions.
- An idol is any idea, ability, possession, or person that you regard more highly than God.
- Pride and arrogance are sure signs you are going down the wrong path—a path that will lead to destruction.

Where to Find It

Elijah transported to heaven . . . . 2 Kings 2:11-12
The ministry of Elisha . . . . 2 Kings 2:13–6:23
The stopped sundial . . . . 2 Kings 20:8-11
The fall of Samaria . . . . .2 Kings 17:5
The fall of Jerusalem . . . . 2 Kings 25

Miracles Performed by Elisha

Elisha's Miracles

- Parts the Jordan River . . . . 2 Kings 2:13-14
- Purifies the water at Jericho . . . . 2 Kings 2:19-22
- Multiplies a widow's oil . . . . 2 Kings 4:1-7
- Raises a boy from the dead . . . . 2 Kings 4:18-37
- Purifies poisonous stew . . . . 2 Kings 4:38-41
- Multiplies prophets' food . . . . 2 Kings 4:42-44
- Heals Naaman's leprosy . . . . 2 Kings 5:1-14
- Condemns Gehazi with leprosy . . . . 2 Kings 5:15-27
- Floats ax head . . . . 2 Kings 6:1-7
- Blinds Syrian army . . . . 2 Kings 6:8-23

The Three Deportations to Babylon

605 B.C.	Daniel and other Jewish youths of nobility taken to Babylon for training (Daniel 1:1-6)
597 B.C.	Ezekiel and others taken captive after the defeat of Jehoiachin (2 Kings 24)
586 B.C.	Jerusalem falls and the last of the survivors are taken to Babylon (2 Kings 25:8-11)

The Kings of the Northern Kingdom of Israel

Jeroboam I	Jehu
Nadab	Jehoahaz
Baasha	Jehoash
Elah	Jeroboam II
Zimri	Zechariah
Tibni	Shallum
Omri	Menahem
Ahab	Pekahiah
Ahaziah	Pekah
Joram	Hoshea

The Kings of the Southern Kingdom of Judah

Rehoboam	Jotham
Abijah	Ahaz
Asa	Hezekiah
Jehoshaphat	Manasseh
Jehoram	Amon
Ahaziah	Josiah
Athaliah (queen)	Jehoahaz
Joash	Jehoiakim
Amaziah	Jehoiachin
Azariah (Uzziah)	Zedekiah

1 Chronicles

So David knew that the LORD
had established him as king over Israel,
for his kingdom was highly exalted
for the sake of His people Israel.
(14:2)

♁

Theme: Israel's spiritual history
Date written: 450–430 B.C.
Author: Ezra
Setting: Israel after the captivity

The books of 1 and 2 Chronicles were originally one book in the Hebrew Bible. They were divided at the time of their translation into Greek, and that division continues into the English translations. First Chronicles covers the same period of Israel's history as the book of 2 Samuel but with one difference. Second Samuel gives a political history of the Davidic dynasty, while 1 Chronicles gives the religious history.

The Skeleton

▸ **Chapters 1–9** *Royal Line of David*

These nine chapters comprise the most comprehensive genealogical tables in the Bible. The first four chapters trace the family tree of David from Adam to Jacob, then through his dynasty during the glory days of the nation, and conclude by giving a list of his descendants who returned from captivity. These chapters demonstrate God's faithfulness in keeping His covenant promises to maintain the Davidic line through the centuries. The next five chapters provide the genealogies of most of the other tribes of Israel.

▸ **Chapters 10–29** *Reign of David*

David's life is presented here in a more positive perspective than in 2 Samuel. Chronicles completely omits David's struggles with Saul, his seven-year reign in Hebron, his various wives, and his son Absalom's rebellion. The most notable omission is his sin with Bathsheba. Because Chronicles is written by priests, the author(s) stresses David's deep spiritual commitment to God and his integrity. Chronicles again reviews God's covenant to establish David's throne, and it emphasizes David's concern for the things of God—especially his desire to build a temple for God. Even though David isn't allowed to build the temple, he spends the rest of the book (chapters 22–29) making preparations for his son, Solomon, to build the temple.

Putting Meat on the Bones

The previous book, 2 Kings, ends with both Israel and Judah in captivity, a dark period in the history of the Jewish people. But with the return of a remnant from exile, the writer(s) of Chronicles wants to unify these newly returned people by summarizing Israel's spiritual history, starting from the very beginning with Adam. It's been over 70 years since the people experienced any form of national unity. If the people could be reminded of their heritage and God's promises to them as a nation, they could gain a greater sense of identity and a vision of their destiny.

Fleshing It Out in Your Life

A review of your spiritual history and God's eternal promises is an important reason for you to read your Bible. Your identity in Christ and God's promises regarding your eternal destiny are in Scripture for your constant review. Also, just as God was faithful to His people in the past by bringing them out of captivity, you can rely on Him to be faithful in the present by protecting and providing for you. You can look ahead with confidence, knowing that God will provide for you and all future generations of believers until His return.

Life Lessons from 1 Chronicles

- God continues to work out His plans in history through His people.
- God will be true to His promises in spite of your checkered past.
- Your past mistakes provide valuable lessons for your present holiness.
- Realize God has a future for you, just as He has a future for Israel.

Where to Find It

Davidic covenant . . . . 1 Chronicles 17:7-27
David's numbering of the people . . . . 1 Chronicles 21:1-13
David's preparations to build the temple . . . . 1 Chronicles 22:1-6
Divisions for the priesthood . . . . .1 Chronicles 24:1

David's Preparations for Building the Temple

- 100,000 talents of gold, approximately 750 tons
- 1,000,000 talents of silver, approximately 37,500 tons
- Bronze and iron beyond measure
- Timber and stone
- Workmen, woodsmen, and stonecutters in abundance

2 Chronicles

If My people who are called by My name will humble themselves, and pray and seek My face, and turn from their wicked ways, then I will hear from heaven, and will forgive their sin and heal their land.
(7:14)

Theme: Israel's spiritual heritage
Date written: 450–430 B.C.
Author: Ezra
Setting: Israel after the exile

The book of 2 Chronicles covers much of the same period as 1 and 2 Kings. Second Chronicles gives a divine editorial on the spiritual nature of the Davidic dynasty from the time of the united kingdom of Solomon to the deportation of the kingdom of Judah; then to the decree of Cyrus, king of Persia, for the exiles to return to Jerusalem and rebuild the temple after a 70-year exile. Because this is a spiritual chronicle of David's lineage, the wicked kings of the northern kingdom and their history are completely omitted.

The Skeleton

▸ **Chapters 1–9** *Solomon's Glory*

A major focus of 1 and 2 Chronicles is the temple. Therefore, much of the last half of 1 Chronicles centers on David's preparation of materials and personnel for the building and the service of the temple. In 2 Chronicles, six of the first nine chapters are devoted to the building and dedication of the temple by Solomon.

▸ **Chapters 10–36** *Judah's Decline and Exile*

The glory of Solomon's temple is short-lived. Soon after Solomon's death, the nation is divided and both kingdoms begin a downward spiral spiritually and politically. The kingdom of Judah, named for its most prominent tribe, must not only battle idolatry and apostasy from within, but also the godless hostility of the northern kingdom and the rising powers of Assyria and Babylonia from without.

This section is a priestly commentary on the 20 kings of Judah. Eight of those kings were good and brought about some level of revival, but the effects of the revivals never lasted beyond one generation. Each successive king is seen with respect to his relationship to the temple as the center of worship and spiritual strength. When the reigning king serves God, the kingdom is blessed, but if or when he forsakes the temple and the worship of God, the nation is torn by warfare and unrest.

Putting Meat on the Bones

One of the central themes of Chronicles is remembrance. The returning remnant is to remember the temple as well as the role of the law and the priesthood. The two books of Chronicles look back to Israel's former glory and offer encouragement to a remnant as they rebuild their heritage. These two books are a history lesson intended to help this present returning generation to remember a very important lesson: The reasons for the decline and fall of the nation are apostasy, idolatry, and intermarriage with their pagan neighbors. Chronicles may have taught the people at least one lesson, for they never again worshipped idols.

Fleshing It Out in Your Life

Like Israel, you are placed on this earth to represent God. But, again like Israel, it's easy to forget who you are and stumble blindly after the idols of wealth, prestige, and fleshly self-fulfillment. If you make anything a higher priority than God, you are worshipping it and not God, despite what you might profess with your lips. It took 70 years of exile to break the Jews of the habit of following after the idols of their neighboring nations. Don't wait for God's hand of judgment; examine your heart and put away any distraction to a wholehearted commitment to and worship of God.

Life Lessons from 2 Chronicles

- There is always a consequence to disobedience.
- You can—and should—learn from the failures of others.
- Yesterday's revival must be renewed today.
- In the same way that the temple was the focal point of worship for Old Testament saints, Christ is to be your focal point today.

Where to Find It

Kings who restored the temple:

Asa .... 2 Chronicles 14:1–16:14
Jehoshaphat .... 2 Chronicles 17:1–20:37
Joash .... 2 Chronicles 24:1-27
Hezekiah .... 2 Chronicles 29–32
Josiah .... 2 Chronicles 34–35

Revival Under Three Good Kings in Judah

Jehoshaphat—When the nation was facing destruction he challenged the people to get serious with God, and disaster was averted (2 Chronicles 20:1-30).

Hezekiah—Purified the temple, destroyed the idols, and brou to God's house (2 Chronicles 29–31).

Josiah—Made a commitment to obey God's Word and rem influences from the land (2 Chronicles 34–35).

Ezra

I was encouraged,
as the hand of the L*ORD my God*
was upon me….
(7:28)

Theme: Restoration
Date written:457–444 B.C.
Author: Ezra
Setting: Jerusalem

Ezra, the author of 1 and 2 Chronicles, picks up where he leaves off at the end of 2 Chronicles. He records the accounts of two returns of a small remnant of Jews from exile. As a priest, Ezra continues his goal of providing a priestly and spiritual perspective on Judah's historical events. In addition, Ezra believes a record of the building of the second temple could be a helpful reminder of the remnant's link to the first temple.

The Skeleton

▸ **Chapters 1–6** *The First Return Under Zerubbabel*

As a priest and a scribe, Ezra draws upon a collection of Persian administrative documents to which he has access to describe the first return to Jerusalem. The book of Ezra opens with the decree repeated from 2 Chronicles from Cyrus, king of Persia, which allowed the people to return to Jerusalem. Ezra lists the families who volunteered to return, tracing their lineage back into Israel's past. This detailed list will help the exiles in years to come reestablish their roots and provide a unifying connection to earlier generations.

Zerubbabel, a direct descendant of King David, heads the list as the leader of those returning. Once the exiles arrive in Jerusalem, Zerubbabel makes the restoration of the altar and the religious feasts his first priority. Next he oversees the laying of the foundation of the temple. But soon opposition arises, and the work is stopped for 14 years. Even in the midst of opposition, the prophets Haggai and Zechariah exhort the people to get back to rebuilding the temple. Zerubbabel and Joshua, the high priest, lead the work, and the second temple is finally completed five years later. In a great celebration the temple is dedicated, the sacrificial offerings are reinstituted, and the people and priests purify themselves, and the Passover is once again observed.

▸ **Chapters 7–10** *The Second Return Under Ezra*

Approximately 60 years after the temple is rebuilt, another king in Persia, Artaxerxes, gives a decree for yet another return of the people. The king authorizes Ezra, a priest and teacher, to lead this group back to Jerusalem. The king and his advisors also include in the decree an offer to Ezra of a large amount of gold and silver to be taken back with him to help beautify the temple. Before leaving Babylon, Ezra and his small group pause and pray and fast for God's protection during the perilous four-month journey.

When the group arrives in Jerusalem, God uses Ezra, a skilled teacher, to rebuild the people spiritually and morally. When Ezra discovers that many of the people have intermarried with foreign women, he offers a great public prayer and pleads with God on their behalf. The people quickly respond and make a covenant to put away their foreign wives and live according to God's law. The book ends with a great revival and changed lifestyles.

Putting Flesh on the Bones

That Ezra had royal administrative documents in hand to support his work in Jerusalem and on the temple conveyed a powerful message when accompanied by Ezra's resounding line "the hand of the LORD my God was upon me" (Ezra 7:6,28). The decrees, proclamations, letters, lists, genealogies, and memoranda, many of them written by the Persian administration, attest to the sovereign hand of God on the two returns of the people to Jerusalem and to Israel's restoration. The primary message of the book of Ezra is that God orchestrated all of what happened during the past grim situation (the captivity) and would continue to work through pagan kings to give Judah hope for the future. God's administration overrides that of any and all of the kings of this world.

Fleshing It Out in Your Life

The book of Ezra is a message of God's continuing covenant grace to Israel as promised in Jeremiah 29:14: "I will bring you back from your captivity; I will gather you from all the nations and from all the places where I have driven you, says the LORD, and I will bring you to the place from which I caused you to be carried away captive." God restored His chosen people from their captivity, and God continues to show His mercy and grace to each new generation of His people. No matter how difficult your present "captivity," you are never far removed from God's love and mercy. Restoration is available each time when you return to Him.

Life Lessons from Ezra

- God always keeps His promises to His people...and to you.
- God is at work behind the scenes to lead and direct your life.
- Strong spiritual leadership is necessary to give people spiritual guidance.
- Preparation to teach God's people is a dedicated undertaking.
- Teaching God's Word will always have a positive effect.

Where to Find It

Zerubbabel, the leader of the first return . . . . Ezra 2:2
Urim and Thummim . . . . Ezra 2:63; Exodus 28:30
The temple work begins . . . . .Ezra 3:8-10
Ezra's preparation for ministry . . . . Ezra 7:10

The Two Returns to Jerusalem in the Book of Ezra

Chapters 1–6	Chapters 7–10
Decreed by Cyrus	Decreed by Artaxerxes
538 B.C.	458 B.C.
Led by Zerubbabel	Led by Ezra
Sacred vessels returned	Gold given for temple
Ministry of the prophets Haggai and Zechariah	Ministry of Ezra
Temple rebuilt	People rebuilt

Nehemiah

Then I said to them, "You see the distress
that we are in, how Jerusalem lies waste,
and its gates are burned with fire.
Come and let us build the wall of Jerusalem,
that we may no longer be a reproach."
(2:17)

Theme: Reconstruction
Date written: 424–400 B.C.
Author: Nehemiah
Setting: Jerusalem

Nehemiah provides a sequel to the narrative of the book of Ezra. First, Ezra arrives on the scene and brings about reforms through the teaching of God's Word. Now 13 years later, Nehemiah, a trusted cupbearer of the king of Persia, arrives in Jerusalem with a burden to rebuild the wall.

In Ezra we were concerned with a two-part problem: The rebuilding of the temple under the leadership of Zerubbabel, and the restoring of worship under the leadership of Ezra. Nehemiah, in turn, is also concerned with a two-part problem: The rebuilding of the walls around Jerusalem (which were destroyed by the Babylonians), and the re-instructing of the Jewish people, who were becoming pagan through intermarriage with the Gentile unbelievers who lived all around them.

The Skeleton

▸ **Chapters 1–7** *Rebuilding the Walls*

The book opens with Nehemiah living in Susa, the winter capital of the Persian king. There he receives reports of the sad living conditions of the people who had volunteered for the first two returns to Jerusalem under Zerubbabel and Ezra. Burdened by these reports, Nehemiah prays and, in the process, realizes he is the best one to help. Therefore, he asks for a leave of absence from his duties as the king's trusted cupbearer, and is given permission by the king to go to Jerusalem as governor of the city.

Upon arriving, Nehemiah inspects the damaged walls and enlists the support of the people, who eagerly begin helping to rebuild the wall. Nehemiah stands ready against the threat of attack from the Ammonites and Arabians by keeping half of the workers armed with weapons while the other half, armed with tools, rebuilds the wall. These enemies did not want to see Jerusalem's walls rebuilt, and they tried to discourage Nehemiah and the workers. But the Jews persisted onward, and a project that had faltered for 70 years was completed in just 52 days! Now that the walls are up, Nehemiah delegates faithful men to have charge over the city and the gates.

▸ **Chapters 8–13** *Re-teaching the People*

With the walls rebuilt and with some measure of protection, the people gather in a great assembly and ask that the law of Moses be brought out and read to them. Ezra, whom we have not heard from for a while, publically reads the law, and the priests and Levites explain the meaning of what is read. The reading lasts from early morning until noon. In response, the people celebrate the Feast of Tabernacles for seven days, and each day Ezra continues to read more of the law. As a further response to God's Word the people fast, put on sackcloth and ashes to demonstrate their humility, separate themselves from the Gentiles around them, confess their sins, and enter into a solemn covenant to observe the ordinances of the law.

Because Jerusalem is now safe and spacious, the population is redistributed so that one out of every ten Jews will live in the city. The others are free to reestablish their family heritage on the land outside the city walls. In a manner similar to the dedication of the rebuilt temple (Ezra 6), the rebuilt walls are dedicated with the music of thanksgiving. Nehemiah is recalled to Persia for an undetermined amount of time.

Nehemiah later returns to Jerusalem and is upset to discover that the high priest has allowed an outsider, a Gentile leader, to have a room in the temple—a flagrant abuse of "the house of God." Nehemiah throws out the man's furniture and cleanses the storage chamber. The book ends with Nehemiah continuing to exhort the leaders to fulfill their earlier covenant with God.

Putting Meat on the Bones

Three major themes can be seen in Nehemiah's account of Israel's struggle to survive in the midst of overwhelmingly hostile odds.

First, the importance of God's Word: There is a constant desire by Israel's leaders to carefully follow God's Word and perform His will. There are several accounts of Ezra and the priests reading from "the Book of the Law of Moses" (8:1) followed by careful explanations of its meaning to the people. The leaders desire to "understand the words of the Law" (8:13) and are so concerned about how the sacrificial system is to be carried out that they are cautious to perform it exactly "as it is written in the Law" (10:34,36). Also, when marriage reforms are needed the leaders act in accordance with what "they read from the Book of Moses" (13:1).

Second, Nehemiah's trust in God: Nehemiah possesses utmost confidence that God is leading and directing his every step. Time and time again Nehemiah attributes his success and preservation to God, referring to "the hand of my God which had been good upon me" (2:18; see also 2:8; 6:16), and saying that "God had brought their plot to nothing" (4:15), and "My God put it into my heart" (7:5).

Third, opposition from Israel's enemies: Just as in Ezra, Judah's enemies try to incite the Persian government to revoke its edicts allowing Judah to rebuild its social and religious system. Yet in spite of corruption and dissension from within Judah and intimidation from the nations around them, Nehemiah and the people rebuild the walls in only 52 days.

Fleshing It Out in Your Life

When it comes to the construction or reconstruction of your spiritual life, follow the example of Nehemiah and the Jews in Jerusalem and remember that God's Word is foundational to your every move. How important is God's Word to the decisions you make? Where does God's truth fit into your building plans? If you want to build a better life, look to God's blueprint.

Nehemiah's trust in God was unshakable. From the day he understood his part in God's plan, his trust in God's provision and protection was unwavering. His confidence was contagious and the people responded by working together to rebuild the city walls. How strong is your trust in God's provision and protection? Trust God in the midst of your difficulties, and your confidence may inspire others toward confidence in God as well.

Finally, make sure you don't underestimate your enemy. Jerusalem's enemies had successfully kept the wall from being rebuilt for 70 years. They had been a formidable opponent! But through prayer and perseverance, the people were watchful, defended themselves, and completed the task. When you face opposition, defend yourself with God's armor (Ephesians 6:14-17) and gain the victory.

Life Lessons from Nehemiah

- At times you may become the answer to your own prayers.
- Most things you do for God's purposes will require acts of faith.
- Don't underestimate the importance of reading and understanding God's Word.
- You must keep a constant vigil against attacks from the enemy of your soul.

Where to Find It

Nehemiah's prayer for Jerusalem .... Nehemiah 1
Nehemiah's request of the king .... Nehemiah 2
The record of the workers .... Nehemiah 3

The attacks of the Samaritans . . . . Nehemiah 4
The cancellation of debt . . . . Nehemiah 5
The completion of the wall in 52 days . . . . Nehemiah 6
The genealogy of the returning Jews . . . . Nehemiah 7
The reading of the law . . . . Nehemiah 8
The people's confession of sin . . . . Nehemiah 9
The people sign a covenant . . . . Nehemiah 10
The list of the leaders . . . . Nehemiah 11
The Levites dedicate the temple . . . . Nehemiah 12
The Levites serve in the temple . . . . Nehemiah 13

Nehemiah's Prayer Life

- When discouraged, he prayed (1:4).
- When seeking direction, he prayed (1:5-11).
- When seeking assistance, he prayed (2:1-5).
- When under attack, he prayed (4:4-5,9).
- When weak and powerless, he prayed (6:9).
- When joyful, he prayed (12:27,43).

Esther

Yet who knows
whether you have come to the kingdom
for such a time as this?
(4:14)

Theme: Preservation
Date: 450–431 B.C.
Author: Unknown
Setting: The court of Persia

The three books of Ezra, Nehemiah, and Esther record God's dealings with the Jews after their prophesied 70 years of captivity in Babylon. While Ezra and Nehemiah deal with the remnant of the people who returned to Judea, the book of Esther deals with the vast majority who decided to stay in the land of their captivity. Esther is one of two books in the Bible given a woman's name, the other being the book of Ruth. Esther is a Jewish girl who by God's sovereignty becomes queen of the vast Persian Empire that stretched from India to Ethiopia. In the midst of a desperate and seemingly hopeless crisis, Queen Esther exerts her influence and the Jewish people are saved from annihilation. Esther's story fits between chapters 6 and 7 of Ezra, and between the first return to Jerusalem led by Zerubbabel and the second return led by Ezra.

The Skeleton

▸ **Chapters 1–5** *The Crisis Anticipated*

The drama opens with Queen Vashti refusing to appear before her husband, King Ahasuerus, at a banquet room filled with drunken men.

She is subsequently banished and an empire-wide search begins for a new queen. Esther, a Jewess, is ultimately selected to become the new queen. Meanwhile, Mordecai, Esther's older cousin, who also raised her, is a government official. Mordecai overhears an assassination plot to kill the king and passes the news on to Esther, who informs the king in Mordecai's name.

Every drama needs a villain, and in the book of Esther, his name is Haman, who is the prime minister, the second in command to the king. Mordecai refuses to bow in reverence to Haman and, in a rage, Haman "cast lots" or "Pur" to determine the best day for the Jews to be slaughtered and eliminated. Once this is done, he asks permission from the king to destroy Mordecai and all the Jews.

Haman deceives the king by describing a "certain people" who are lawless and deserve to die. The king, not knowing who the people are but eager to eliminate any people who are rebellious, issues an edict condemning the Jews to death. Because Esther has never revealed her Jewish heritage, the king has unwittingly approved the killing of his own queen! When Mordecai tells Queen Esther about the edict, she determines to risk her life to save her people. Esther then plans a banquet and invites the king and Haman, hoping for an opportunity to expose Haman's evil plot.

▸ **Chapters 6–10** *The Crisis Overruled*

The night before Esther's banquet, the king is unable to sleep and asks for records from the royal archives to be read to him. While the records are being read, the king learns that some time ago Mordecai had uncovered a plot against him, an act for which Mordecai had not been rewarded. The next morning the king asks Haman what should be done to properly honor a hero. Haman thinks the king must be talking about him, so he describes a lavish and public reward. The king then tells Haman to honor Mordecai in this way.

Things go from bad to worse for Haman as Esther reveals that she is a Jew and exposes Haman's plot. In a fury, the king has Haman hanged on the gallows that Haman had prepared for the hanging of Mordecai. The king then gives a new edict that allows the Jews in all the provinces to defend themselves against the attacks which Haman's proclamation had authorized. To celebrate this historic occasion, the Feast of Purim was established and is still celebrated among Jewish people today. In the final act of this true-life drama, Mordecai is appointed to take Haman's place as prime minister.

Putting Meat on the Bones

The preservation of God's people was accomplished through a beauty contest, a pagan king, and a courageous woman. Furthermore, regardless of whether the individual Jewish people had chosen to return to Jerusalem or remain in Persia, God protected them. The preservation of those who remained was not dependent on the Persian Empire or their possessions or positions, but on God's plan for and promises to His people. God worked through one woman who was willing to risk her life for her people. When she realized the need for her to take a stand, she uttered the famous words, "If I perish, I perish!" (4:16).

Though God's name does not appear even once in the book of Esther, the clear message that emerges from its pages is that God is totally sovereign over all things. He faithfully guided and protected His covenant people and overruled human schemes on their behalf, regardless of whether they lived in Shushan, the capital of Persia, or were scattered in one of the 127 Persian provinces that stretched from India to Ethiopia.

Fleshing It Out in Your Life

How much of your security do you think lies in your possessions, position, reputation, or place of residence? Wherever you live and whatever you possess, realize God did not place you there or give you those things for your own benefit. No, He has put you there and provided you with the means to serve Him. Esther did not choose to be in King Ahasuerus's palace nor to be his queen. But in her position there, God used her mightily to preserve His people. Regardless of what you have or don't have, whether your circumstances are considered good or bad, God can and will protect you. And He can and will use you to help His people. You may not see His mighty hand of provision and protection, but be assured, He is at work on your behalf. He is your ultimate security and provision, and He will take care of you.

Life Lessons from Esther

- Don't let less-than-perfect circumstances keep you from trusting in God.
- Don't think that a difficult life prevents you from great service to God and His people.
- God's protective hand is always present even though it is not always visible.
- It takes courage to speak up for your beliefs and be willing to suffer the consequences of doing so.
- Each of God's people—including you—has been prepared by God for some purpose and strategic usefulness.

Where to Find It

Mordecai's discovery of a plot against the king .... Esther 2:21-23
Haman's plot against the Jews .... Esther 3:8-9
Mordecai's statement, "For such a time as this" Esther 4:14
Esther's decision, "If I perish, I perish!" .... Esther 4:16
Haman's death on his own gallows .... Esther 7:10
Institution of the Feast of Purim .... Esther 9:20-24

The Feast of Purim

- The first and only non-Mosaic festival
- An annual two-day holiday of rejoicing
- Held in February or March
- Named for the Akkadian word for *lot*

The Poetic Books

♁

The 17 historical books which comprise the first portion of the Old Testament are concluded. They gave the history of civilization from creation to the time of the Persian Empire. They record the history of the Jewish nation from its inception through its days of glory and deportation, and finally, to its days of survival as a small, insignificant nation surrounded by enemies intent on destroying it.

Now comes a different set of books, which are known as the poetic books of the Bible: Job, Psalms, Proverbs, Ecclesiastes, and the Song of Solomon. They don't relate historical experiences. Rather they relate the experiences of the human heart. They do not advance the story of the nation of Israel. Instead, through the use of Hebrew poetry, they delve into the questions of suffering, wisdom, life, love, and most importantly, the character and nature of God. And finally, they have another important function—they serve as a hinge linking the history of the past with the prophetic books of the future.

Job

I abhor myself,
and repent in dust and ashes.
(42:6)

Theme: Blessings through suffering
Date written: 2000–1800 B.C.
Author: Unknown
Setting: Land of Uz

The book of Job is considered by many Bible scholars to be the oldest book in the Bible. Job probably lived during the same time period as Abraham. Like Abraham, Job is a wealthy and upright man who fears God. This book that bears Job's name describes the death of his self-righteousness. Through the fires of affliction—which include the loss of his family, his wealth, and his health—a series of debates takes place with his friends over the subject of suffering. Then in a discussion with God, Job is brought to the end of questioning God's actions in his life and trying to justify himself. He finally grasps the greatness, majesty, sovereignty, and utter independence of God and he sees himself as God sees him. He repents of his arrogance, and God restores his health, gives him another family, and makes him more wealthy than before.

The Skeleton

▸ **Chapters 1–3** *The Drama*

The book of Job opens with the facts of Job's integrity, his wealth, and his children. He does not seem like a good candidate for disaster. But in a rare glimpse into the halls of heaven, Satan is seen as the accuser, charging that no one, including Job, loves God from pure motives. Satan claims that people love God only for material blessings. To refute Satan's accusations, God allows Satan to strike Job with two series of disasters. The first takes his wealth and his family, and the second takes his health. Job's wife sees his suffering and tells him to "curse God and die." Four friends hear of Job's adversities and come to give a measure of sympathy. For seven days they sit before Job, watching his suffering. At the end of the seven days, Job breaks the silence by repeatedly lamenting the day of his birth.

▸ **Chapters 4–37** *The Debates*

After Job breaks the silence, three rounds of debates follow with Job's friends. Their charges all have the same theme: Job is suffering because of some deep, dark sin in his life. Having no knowledge of God's discussions with Satan, his friends believe that confession is the only cure. With each round of accusations—and Job's repeated denials—the emotional fervor of the argument increases. Job first accuses his friends of judging him, which they are. Finally out of frustration at the repeated accusations, Job appeals to God as his judge. Job's defenses are much longer than his friends' accusations, and in the process of defending his innocence, he becomes guilty of arrogant self-righteousness. After Job gives a five-chapter closing argument claiming his innocence, Elihu, the fourth friend, who has been silent thus far, gives a more accurate view of Job's problem than the other three friends did. Elihu suggests Job needs to humble himself before God and submit to God's work of purifying his life through trials.

▸ **Chapters 38–42** *The Deliverance*

After Elihu's speech, God ends the debate by speaking to Job out of a whirlwind. God gives two speeches. In the first, He reveals His power and wisdom as Creator and Sustainer of the physical and animal world. Job could only acknowledge his ignorance and insignificance.

In the second speech, God describes His sovereign authority and power. Job responds by acknowledging his error with a repentant heart. If he couldn't understand God's workings in the natural realm, how could he possibly understand God's ways in the supernatural realm?

Job finally understands his suffering from God's perspective. Satan's challenge had become God's opportunity to build Job's faith and character. And in the end, God restored twofold all that Job had initially possessed.

Putting Meat on the Bones

The book of Job is a fascinating story of riches-to-rags-to-riches. It provides insights into the problem of suffering, the certainty of divine sovereignty, the activities of Satan, and a faith that endures. Job was tested, and his faith endured because it was built on the firm foundation of God. His affliction initially caused him to complain, and his self-examination produced a growing self-righteousness. But Job's repentance from his error led to his restoration. In the end, his trial brought about an amazing transformation. Job was a different man after he graduated from God's school of suffering. And in defense of Job's friends, though his "comforters" may have come to wrong conclusions about his suffering, they were the only people who came to his side in his time of need. And Elihu's final speech is never rebuked, which confirms his more accurate understanding of Job's problem and God's solution.

Fleshing It Out in Your Life

God is all-wise and all-powerful, and His will is perfect. However, in our finite minds, you and I don't always understand His actions. Suffering doesn't make sense to us. After all, we wrongly wonder, aren't God's people supposed to prosper, to always receive blessings and enjoy a sorrow-free life? In our misunderstanding of God, we, like Job, despair. We question God, and at times we even shake our fist at Him in frustration. Job teaches us there are many things we will never understand, including suffering. But one thing we do know: God is never insensitive to our suffering. His sufficiency makes up for our insufficiency, and, in the end, we are drawn closer to Him.

Life Lessons from Job

- Spiritual affairs are going on in heaven that you know nothing about, yet they affect your life.
- Life issues cannot always be understood in human terms.
- God's people do suffer. Bad things do happen to good people.
- You cannot always judge a person's spirituality by his or her pain or prosperity.
- God always has a reason for what you are asked to endure.
- Suffering should improve your worship as you draw closer to God and His comfort.

Where to Find It

Satan's debates with God . . . . Job 1:6–2:10
Friends' debates with Job . . . . Job 4–37
God's questions to Job . . . . Job 38–41
Job's confession to God . . . . Job 42
God's blessing of Job . . . . Job 42

Some Sources of Suffering

- The fall of man—Genesis 3:16-19
- The consequences of your sins—Galatians 6:7
- The sins of others—Genesis 37:26-28
- Unavoidable consequences—Luke 10:30
- Unavoidable disaster—Luke 13:1-5
- Consequence of your beliefs—Philippians 1:29; 2 Timothy 3:12
- God's greater plan—Job 1:1–2:13

Psalms

My mouth shall speak the praise of the LORD,
and all flesh shall bless
His holy name forever and ever.
(145:21)

Theme: Praise
Date written: 1410–450 B.C.
Author: Various authors
Setting: Heaven and earth

The Psalms are poetic expressions of human and religious feeling, and are divided into five books that comprise a total of 150 individual psalms. The Psalms span the ten centuries from Moses to the days after the Jewish people's exile. They consist of a wide variety of styles and purposes and emotions, such as lament, thanksgiving, praise, worship, pilgrimage, petition, and penitence. Each of the five books ends with a doxology. The last psalm is the closing psalm for book five and for the book of Psalms as a whole.

The Skeleton

▸ **Chapters 1–41** *Book One*

David is designated as being the author of almost half of the psalms (73 of the 150 psalms). He authored all the psalms in this first book or grouping of psalms. David's wide range of experiences as a shepherd, musician, warrior, and king are reflected in his psalms. The psalms in this grouping are basically songs of praise and worship. The most well-known psalm in this section is Psalm 23, which begins with the familiar and well-loved words, "The LORD is my shepherd" (Psalm 23:1). A prophetic description of the "suffering Messiah" can be found in Psalm 22.

▸ **Chapters 42–72** *Book Two*

David and the sons of Korah (a group of singers and composers) account for most of the psalms in book two. Many of the psalms in this grouping are hymns of national interest and describe God's nature and His judgment of the wicked and deliverance of the righteous. David's public song of repentance after his sinful affair with Bathsheba is located in this section. In it, David cries out, "Have mercy upon me, O God, according to Your lovingkindness" (Psalm 51:1). These psalms help us reserve a sense of wonder and thankfulness toward God in our worship.

▸ **Chapters 73–89** *Book Three*

Asaph was appointed by David as a leader of one of the temple choirs (1 Chronicles 25:1), and is the author of the majority of the psalms in this section. This group of "songs" celebrates the sovereignty of God, God's hand in history, His faithfulness, and His covenant with David. These psalms remind us that the worship of our great God should be continual. The psalmist declared, "I will sing of the mercies of the LORD forever; with my mouth will I make known Your faithfulness to all generations" (Psalm 89:1).

▸ **Chapters 90–106** *Book Four*

Although five of these psalms are attributed to David, most of them were written anonymously. Primarily these psalms are anthems of praise and reflection, and a prayer by Moses is the opening psalm in this section. Moses reminds us that our time on this earth is limited and we are to use it wisely. He tells us to "number our days, that we may gain a heart of wisdom" (Psalm 90:12).

▸ **Chapters 107–150** *Book Five*

Many of these psalms are attributed to David, and many are anthems of praise. They exalt God's works, recount the blessings of righteous living, and the longest psalm (Psalm 119) praises God for His wonderful Word. The poetry in this grouping reminds us that the most perfect sacrifice we can offer to God is a faithful and obedient life.

Putting Meat on the Bones

Even though Psalms is made up of a variety of psalms written by different authors over the course of hundreds of years, they are wonderfully unified by their common theme of worship—the worship of God for who He is, what He has done, and what He will do in the future. God's goodness extends through all time and eternity. These anthems and songs of praise were written with refreshing honesty and transparency. In them we see the psalmists share their deepest feelings for and with God.

Within the Psalms is a group of psalms collectively referred to as the "imprecatory psalms," meaning they "call down a curse." These psalms give some people a problem, as they seem to be harsh and unloving. But here are a few things to keep in mind as you ponder the imprecatory psalms: First, they are in the Bible and are therefore of divine origin. Next, these psalms call for divine justice, not human vengeance. Also, they call upon God to punish the wicked and thus vindicate His righteousness. Finally, even Jesus called down a curse on the inhabitants of several cities that rejected the gospel. Summed up, God is the God of love, but He is also the God of justice.

Fleshing It Out in Your Life

The Psalms focus on God and reflect His program for His people. The more you read them, the more you understand and are blessed by what you learn of God and His work as Creator, Redeemer, Sustainer, and Comforter. Like the psalmists, you should be moved to praise and worship the Lord. The Psalms can help continually guide you into a deeper and more meaningful relationship with God.

Life Lessons from the Psalms

- The Psalms give you a better understanding of God.
- The Psalms can guide you in your ongoing relationship with God.
- The Psalms are a source of comfort in times of pain and distress.
- The Psalms remind you often of God's control over all things.
- The Psalms provide a model for praise and worship.

Where to Find It

The psalm of the cross .... Psalm 22
The Shepherd's psalm .... Psalm 23
David's psalms of repentance .... Psalm 32; 51
Moses' psalm .... Psalm 90
A psalm about God's Word .... Psalm 119
Songs of ascents to Jerusalem .... Psalm 120–134

The Message of the Psalms

Let everything that has breath praise the LORD.
Praise the LORD!
(Psalm 150:6)

Proverbs

The fear of the Lord
is the beginning of knowledge,
but fools despise wisdom and instruction.
(1:7)

Theme: Practical wisdom
Date written: 971–686 B.C.
Author: Primarily Solomon
Setting: Everyday life

While David is the author of a majority of the psalms, his son, Solomon, is the author of most of the book of Proverbs. Early in his rule, Solomon was granted great wisdom by God (1 Kings 4:29-34). Much of his wisdom is reflected in the 800 proverbs that are included in the book of Proverbs.

A *proverb* can be described as a brief statement that offers a pithy but powerful observation. And it is common for proverbs to use comparisons, contrasts, analogies, or figures of speech to help drive home their point. The book of Proverbs is the most practical book in the Old Testament because it gives simple illustrations and insights about the basic realities of everyday life. The object of Proverbs is to inspire profound reverence for God, a fear of His judgments, and a deep love for wisdom and godly living. The book of Proverbs is meant to be to your practical life what the book of Psalms is to your devotional life.

The Skeleton

▸ **Chapters 1–9** *Wisdom for Young People*

After a brief introduction that spells out the purpose and theme of the book of Proverbs—to instruct in wisdom and to help in the acquisition of discernment—Solomon enlightens the young men of his day like a father giving advice to his sons. He gives a series of ten exhortations, each beginning with the impassioned plea, "My son." Solomon challenges young men (and women) to treasure wisdom above all else. Wisdom, he explains, will help them avoid crime and evil people, provide freedom and safety, give discernment on how to shun immorality and keep from living foolishly. Anyone beginning—and continuing—their journey to discover more wisdom will benefit from these wise sayings. Solomon's goal is "to give prudence to the simple, to the young man [or woman] knowledge and discretion" (Proverbs 1:4).

▸ **Chapters 10–24** *Wisdom for All People*

Solomon wants to impart wisdom not only to the youth of his day, but also to all people, regardless of age, sex, or position in society. This section contains a collection of proverbs from Solomon and a number of lessons from other wise men. These short sayings give practical wisdom for daily living. They contrast good and evil, right and wrong, impart advice on child-raising, money matters, and speech. Ultimately, "every prudent man acts with knowledge, but a fool lays open his folly" (Proverbs 13:16).

▸ **Chapters 25–29** *Wisdom for Leaders*

According to 1 Kings 4:32, Solomon spoke 3000 proverbs and 1005 songs. This section of Proverbs contains more of these proverbs, collected by the men serving under King Hezekiah. While most of these sayings are general in nature, many are directed toward the king and those who deal with him. They are useful for those who are leaders or aspire to be leaders in any area of life—at home, at church, at school, in the government, and on the job. Solomon instructs, "It is the glory of God to conceal a matter, but the glory of kings [or leaders] is to search out a matter" (Proverbs 25:2).

▸ **Chapters 30–31** *Wisdom for Disciples*

The last two chapters of Proverbs act almost as an appendix of sayings by two unknown sages. The first unknown sage is Agur. He gives his advice to two of his disciples, Itiel and Ucal, in clusters of numerical proverbs—"Two things I request of You.... There are three things that are never satisfied.... There are three things which are too wonderful for me" (Proverbs 30:7,15,18). The last chapter of Proverbs contains wisdom passed on from a wise mother to her disciple—her son, King Lemuel. In the first part of Proverbs 31, the mother advises her son on how to be a good king. In the remaining verses, she asks the question, "Who can find a virtuous wife?" (Proverbs 31:10), and then gives her son advice on what to look for in a good wife.

Putting Meat on the Bones

Solomon came to the throne with great promise, privilege, and opportunity. God granted him wisdom beyond any other man of his day. In the first part of his reign, Solomon was sought out by kings and queens, by the common folk and upper levels of society alike for his wise counsel. It is assumed that Solomon wrote most of his wisdom proverbs during those early years of devotion to God. But amazingly and tragically, Solomon failed to live out the truths that he knew and wrote about in his later years. He became the fool that he so ardently taught against in Proverbs!

Fleshing It Out in Your Life

As you read Proverbs, understand well Solomon's message that knowing God is the key to wisdom. Then read the rest of God's Word to gain more of God's wisdom. Listen to the thoughts and lessons from not only the world's wisest man, Solomon, but also from the Bible's many other teachers. Review these truths repeatedly and apply them always in your life. "The fear of the LORD is the beginning of wisdom, and the knowledge of the Holy One is understanding" (Proverbs 9:10).

Life Lessons from Proverbs

- Chose God's ways. He will lead you into making right decisions.
- Chose your words carefully. They reveal your inner character.
- Chose to work diligently. God will be honored, and you will profit and gain skills in your labors.
- Chose your friends carefully. They are a reflection of you.
- Chose to develop moral character and devotion to God. This is success in God's eyes.

Where to Find It

Wisdom .... Proverbs 2:6; 18:15
Discipline (self-control) Proverbs15:18; 16:32; 25:28
Speech .... Proverbs 16:23-24; 21:23
Friends .... Proverbs 17:17; 18:24; 22:24-25
Money .... Proverbs 3:9; 11:28; 13:11
Food .... Proverbs 30:7-9
Parenting .... Proverbs 20:15; 22:6

A Father's Instruction on the Value of Wisdom from Proverbs 3:1-26

- Wisdom is established in sound teaching.
- Wisdom will add health and peace to your life.
- Wisdom finds favor with God and man.
- Wisdom looks to God and fears.
- Wisdom looks to God for understanding.
- Wisdom generates strength.
- Wisdom welcomes chastening for its benefits.
- Wisdom is better than gold.
- Wisdom is seen in creation.
- Wisdom will keep you on the right path.

Ecclesiastes

Fear God and keep His commandments,
for this is man's all.
(12:13)

Theme: All is vanity apart from God
Date written: 940–931 B.C.
Author: Solomon
Setting: The end of Solomon's life

The title for this next and fourth book in the wisdom series is *Ecclesiastes,* meaning "an official speaker in an assembly." In the case of Ecclesiastes, it is one speaker, "the Preacher" (Ecclesiastes 1:1). There is no doubt this book is an autobiography written by King Solomon at the end of his life after he strayed away from God. As if he were reporting the results of a scientific experiment, Solomon, the Preacher, shares his search for satisfaction. In four "sermons," he relates his discovery that life without God is a long and fruitless search for enjoyment, meaning, and fulfillment. Solomon hopes to spare his readers the bitterness of learning through personal experience that carrying out life's pursuits apart from God is empty, hollow, fruitless, and meaningless.

The Skeleton

▸ **Chapters 1–2** *Solomon's Personal Experiences*

The Preacher describes his experiential quest for meaning and satisfaction as he explores his vast personal resources. He moves from wisdom to laughter, hedonism, and from wine to works, women, and wealth. But all lead to emptiness. He concludes by acknowledging that contentment and joy are found only in God.

▸ **Chapters 3–5** *Solomon's General Observations*

The Preacher now moves from his personal experiences to general observations about the world and human activity. He finds himself up against what seems to be divine providence—an apparently immutable fixed state for all that happens. He considers the unchanging order of events and concludes, "There is a time for every purpose under heaven"—a truth that cannot be understood but needs to be accepted (Ecclesiastes 3:1). Solomon looks next at human oppression, inequality, popularity, wealth, and honor, and again arrives at a similar conclusion: "In the multitude of dreams and many words there is also vanity. But fear God" (Ecclesiastes 5:7).

▸ **Chapters 6–8** *Solomon's Practical Counsel*

The Preacher is moving toward his conclusion. The secret mankind is looking for lies in finding the true center of conduct. In achieving the even balance in life, the proper poise in behavior, the correct middle-course for living, Solomon gives an interim conclusion that a man or woman should "eat, drink, and be merry; for this will remain with him in his labor all the days of his life which God gives him under the sun" (Ecclesiastes 8:15).

▸ **Chapters 8–12** *Solomon's Final Conclusion*

When we look at our lives, we are tempted to find them meaningless and empty. All our endeavors seem fruitless and transitory, and all our pleasures and attainments fail to bring true fulfillment. The one thing we can know with certainty is that we will die. The only thing that can help us overcome our hopelessness and achieve true meaning in life is to acknowledge and obey our Creator.

Putting Meat on the Bones

Although the tone of Ecclesiastes is negative and pessimistic—"vanity of vanities, all is vanity"—no reader should conclude that the only chapter worth reading and applying is the last one, which gives Solomon's ultimate and positive conclusions. The entire book was inspired by the Holy Spirit, making the entire book a vital source of practical wisdom. Consider, for instance, Ecclesiastes 3:1-8, a famous passage that teaches us "everything has its time." Take to heart, too, the Preacher's instruction on spiritual wisdom—"Fear God and keep His commandments, for this is man's all" (Ecclesiastes 12:13).

Fleshing It Out in Your Life

All Solomon's remarks are preserved in the book of Ecclesiastes for a purpose—to lead you to seek true happiness in God alone. Solomon is not trying to destroy all your hopes. He is instead directing them to the only One who can truly fulfill them. Solomon affirms the value of knowledge, relationships, work, and pleasure, but shows us that their value is realized only in their proper place of priority in the light of eternity.

Life Lessons from Ecclesiastes

- All your activities in life should be seen and measured in the light of eternity.
- Nothing in this life will bring true meaning and happiness—not wealth, fame, pleasure, or success. Only in God can you find real fulfillment.
- There is much less that you can depend on than you might think!
- True happiness comes only from obedience to God.

Where to Find It

"Vanity of vanities" . . . . Ecclesiastes 1:2
"There is nothing new under the sun" . . . . Ecclesiastes 1:9
"To everything there is a season" . . . . Ecclesiastes 3:1-8
"Whatever your hand finds to do,
do it with your might" . . . . Ecclesiastes 9:10
"Remember now your Creator in the days
of your youth" . . . . Ecclesiastes 12:1

All Is Vanity

V anity of godless living
A ccumulating wealth
N ot heeding God's authority
I gnoring God's timing
T rusting the wisdom of man
Y earning for pleasure

Song of Solomon

My beloved is mine, and I am his.
(2:16)

♁

Theme: Love and marriage
Date written: 971–965 B.C.
Author: Solomon
Setting: Early in Solomon's reign

This is the final of three books written by Solomon, all included in the Bible's wisdom books. Look at these three books with this in mind: Ecclesiastes is written in Solomon's old age as he reflects back on his life. The majority of Proverbs is written in the maturity of Solomon's life when his focus is still on God and on sharing God's wisdom with others. Now, in Song of Solomon, a youthful Solomon is writing a wedding song to describe his love for and marriage to a beautiful country girl called the "Shulamite" (Song of Solomon 6:13). This song records the dialogue between an ordinary Jewish maiden and her "beloved," the king of Israel.

The Skeleton

▸ **Chapters 1–3** *The Courtship*

This "song" opens at the wedding banquet as the bride thinks about how much she loves her groom, recalling how they first met, the longing she feels toward him, and all the wonderful romantic memories they shared in their courtship. She recalls her anticipation of her beloved's arrival to take her to Jerusalem for the wedding. As she muses, there are brief interludes from Solomon and a choir of young women called the "daughters of Jerusalem" (see, for example, 1:5).

▸ **Chapters 3–5:1** *The Wedding Preparation*

In this section, the king does the majority of the speaking. He comes for his bride, in all his splendor, and brings her to Jerusalem. As his bride spoke with admiration and desire for her groom in the earlier chapters, so Solomon speaks with poetic beauty of his bride in this section as he anticipates their union. The wedding takes place, and the couple consummate their union.

▸ **Chapters 5:2–8** *The Marriage*

Some time after the wedding, the Shulamite is half-awakened from her sleep by her husband's unexpected return home and his desire to give her a romantic surprise. When she fully realizes that she is not dreaming and gets up to let him in, he is gone. She panics and desperately tries to find him. She asks the "daughters of Jerusalem" to help her find him. They ask her to remember how special he is, which she gladly does. Later the two find each other, and they spend the remainder of the book singing each other's praises and asserting their unquenchable love for each other.

Putting Meat on the Bones

The world wants to distort what God has created and pronounced as good. Sex has been twisted, exploited, and turned into an illicit, casual, and self-gratifying activity. Love has turned to lust, giving has been exchanged for getting, and the commitment of marriage is shunned in favor of "living together." Fortunately, this tender poetic marriage song gives God's perspective on love, sex, and marriage. It celebrates the joy and intimacy that make up a romantic relationship between a husband and wife. It gives a passionate picture of physical love within the sanctity of marriage. It reveals the importance of verbally communicating love to a spouse. So beautiful is the affection described between this husband and wife that many Bible scholars have drawn a parallel with the great love Jesus Christ shows for His bride, the church.

Fleshing It Out in Your Life

This book of inspired poetry can give you a model of God's intentions for love and marriage. Love is a powerful expression of feeling and commitment between two people. Love doesn't just look for outward physical beauty. It looks for the inner qualities that never fade with time—spiritual commitment, integrity, sensitivity, and sincerity. Therefore, such love is not to be regarded in a casual manner, and the physical expression of this kind of true love should be withheld until marriage. And after marriage, it is this genuine, internal love that won't let walls come between you and your spouse. It is a love that is careful to communicate, reconcile, renew, and refresh.

Life Lessons from the Song of Solomon

- God takes great joy in the passionate romantic love between a husband and wife.
- A couple should openly express their love and admiration for each other.
- Marriage, with all its misunderstandings, is a work in progress.
- A husband and wife honor God when they love and enjoy each other.
- Christ's love for His church is similar to the kind of passion that the bride and groom had for one another.

Where to Find It

The couple's courtship . . . . Song of Solomon 1:2–3:5
The couple's first night as husband and wife . . . . Song of Solomon 4:1–5:1
The couple's first disagreement . . . . Song of Solomon 5:2–6:3
The power of love . . . . Song of Solomon 8:6-7

Help for Husbands and Wives

1. Leave others and cleave to one another . . . . Genesis 2:24
2. Be faithful to your mate . . . . Proverbs 5:15
3. Remember that two are better than one . . . . Ecclesiastes 4:9-10
4. Live together joyfully . . . . Ecclesiastes 9:9
5. Honor and prefer one another. . . . . Romans 12:10
6. The marriage bed is undefiled . . . . Hebrews 13:4
7. Remember you are heirs together of the grace of life. . . . . 1 Peter 3:7

The Prophetic Books

♁

The next 17 books of the Bible comprise about one-fourth of the Scriptures and make up the last division in the Old Testament—the Prophets. The office of *prophet* was instituted during the days of Samuel, and those who were prophets stood along with the priests as God's special representatives. The men who wrote these books were called or appointed to "speak for" God Himself. God communicated His messages to them through a variety of means, including dreams, visions, angels, nature, miracles, and an audible voice. Unfortunately, the messages they shared from God were often rejected and their lives endangered. The prophetic books have four major themes and purposes:

1. To expose the sinful practices of the people
2. To call the people back to the moral, civil, and ceremonial law of God
3. To warn the people of coming judgment
4. To anticipate the coming of Messiah

Isaiah

All we like sheep have gone astray;
we have turned, every one, to his own way;
and the L*ORD has laid on Him*
the iniquity of us all.
(53:6)

Theme: Salvation
Date written: 700–680 B.C.
Author: Isaiah
Setting: Mainly in Jerusalem

The book of Isaiah is the first of the writings of the prophets. Isaiah is generally considered to be the greatest prophet. His ministry spanned the reigns of four kings of Judah. He was raised in an aristocratic home and married to a prophetess. He was initially well liked, but, like most of the other prophets, was soon despised because his messages were so harsh and confrontive. In the first 39 chapters Isaiah stresses the righteousness, holiness, and justice of God. It is interesting to note that the Old Testament also has 39 books. The last 27 chapters of Isaiah portray the Lord's glory, compassion, and grace—a similar theme in the 27 books of the New Testament.

The Skeleton

▸ **Chapters 1–12** *Judgment Upon Judah*

The spiritual condition of Israel has deteriorated to the point that the people are offering child sacrifices. Though the people profess to be religious, their hearts are corrupt and they engage in idolatry. Isaiah repeatedly warns Israel and Judah of coming judgment if the people do not turn from their evil ways.

▸ **Chapters 13–24** *Judgment Upon the Nations*

One of the key reasons for Israel's spiritual downfall is that the people are imitating the wicked lifestyles of those who live in the surrounding nations. Warnings are given against Babylon, Philistia, Moab, Egypt, and Ethiopia, among others. In carrying out judgment against the sins of the nations, God affirms His sovereign rule over all the earth. Ultimately justice will be done, and no one can escape.

▸ **Chapters 25–35** *Judgment and Redemption*

Near the midpoint of the book, Isaiah begins to intersperse words of hope alongside words of condemnation. God reveals the first glimpses of His plan to call His people back to Him and restore them.

▸ **Chapters 36–39** *Interlude with Hezekiah*

In the midst of Isaiah's powerful declarations of coming judgment is an inspiring story about Hezekiah, a king of Judah (the southern kingdom). At first Hezekiah listens to Isaiah's advice to trust God when Judah is threatened by the Assyrian army. Sure enough, God intervenes and destroys the enemy. Later, when Hezekiah becomes severely ill, Isaiah warns that he would not recover. The king begs God for mercy, and God gives him 15 more years of life.

▸ **Chapters 40–66** *Redemption and Future Glory*

Though judgment upon God's people is imminent and will be severe, that is not the end of the story. The people can count on God's promise to one day restore and deliver them. God will freely forgive all those who repent of their sin, and Isaiah predicts Israel's eventual repentance and its restoration to glory.

Putting Meat on the Bones

The basic theme of this book is found in Isaiah's name, which means "salvation is of the Lord." The word "salvation" appears 26 times in Isaiah, but only 7 times in all the other prophets combined. In the first 39 chapters of Isaiah, man is pictured as being in great need of salvation—a salvation that is of God, not man. Isaiah describes God as the supreme Ruler, the sovereign Lord of history, and man's only Savior. Then in a dramatic shift, the last 27 chapters portray God as being faithful to His covenant by preserving a godly remnant and providing salvation and deliverance through the coming Messiah. The fact that the Messiah is to be both a suffering servant and a sovereign Lord would not be understood until Jesus' time on earth. This Savior is to come out of Judah and will accomplish redemption and restoration with universal blessing for both Jews and Gentiles in His future kingdom.

Fleshing It Out in Your Own Life

God's judgment is coming, and you too need a Savior. You cannot save yourself. Christ's perfect sacrifice for your sins is foretold and pictured in Isaiah. Just as Isaiah foretold, Christ came in the flesh and paid the price for sin in His death. With His resurrection, He is now willing to save all those who turn from their sin and come to Him. Have you committed yourself to Him? If you have experienced His salvation, continue to be faithful and live in anticipation of His soon return.

Life Lessons from Isaiah

- God is a holy God. He cannot overlook sin.
- God knows the future. His judgment, as predicted in Isaiah, was fulfilled perfectly.
- God is a God of love. He is gracious and forgives you when you repent.
- God always keeps His promises. He will fulfill His plan for you, and for Israel's future salvation.
- The prophecies about Christ's suffering on the cross were accurately fulfilled and Christ's work made it possible for you to enter into God's forever family.

Where to Find It

Prediction of Jesus' birth . . . . Isaiah 7:14
Hezekiah's sickness and recovery . . . . Isaiah 38
Description of the suffering servant . . . . Isaiah 49–57
Prophecy of Christ's death on the cross . . . . Isaiah 53
The wolf and lamb will feed together . . . . Isaiah 65:25

Description of Christ and His Suffering in Isaiah 53

Verse 2—Unattractive and undesirable
Verse 3—Despised and rejected, a man of sorrows
Verse 4—Bore our grief and sorrows
Verse 5—Wounded, bruised, and beaten for our transgressions
Verse 6—Bore the guilt and sin of all
Verse 7—Like a lamb brought to the slaughter
Verse 8—Tried and led away to His death
Verse 9—Died with the wicked but buried with the rich
Verse 10—Suffered according to God's good plan
Verse 12—Poured out His soul unto death and was counted as a sinner

Jeremiah

Now therefore, amend your ways and your doings,
and obey the voice of the LORD your God;
then the LORD will relent concerning the doom
that He has pronounced against you.
(26:13)

Theme: Judgment
Date: 627–586 B.C.
Author: Jeremiah
Setting: Jerusalem

Some 80 to 100 years after Isaiah's death, Jeremiah enters the prophetic scene. The book of Jeremiah is an autobiography of Jeremiah's life and ministry during the reigns of the last five kings of Judah. Jeremiah is the last prophet before the fall of Jerusalem. He is called "the weeping prophet" because of his deep sorrow over the unrepentant nation, the upcoming destruction of Jerusalem, and the exile of its people. Jeremiah is a picture of faithfulness to God and great personal sacrifice in spite of unimaginable opposition. Jeremiah proclaims not only words of warning, but also words of encouragement as he affirms God's promises to renew His people by renewing their hearts.

The Skeleton

▸ **Chapter 1** *God's Call on Jeremiah*

Jeremiah is called and set apart to be God's prophet even before his birth. This opening chapter identifies the prophet, documents his commissioning by God, and outlines his instructions and the protection that God would give him.

▸ **Chapters 2–45** *God's Judgment on Judah*

Jeremiah's messages are communicated through a variety of parables and object lessons. Some are proclaimed in the temple, and others are declared in the streets. The prophet's own life also serves as a daily reminder of the coming judgment of Judah. He is told by God to cut off his hair, to bury a linen sash, to not marry and have a family, to place two baskets of figs—one good and the other bad—before the temple, and to wear a yoke throughout the city. All these visuals are meant to warn the people of imminent judgment if the nation does not repent.

Because Jeremiah's message goes unheeded, judgment does come upon Judah in chapter 39, and the city is destroyed. The Jews who flee the destruction of the city take Jeremiah to Egypt against his will. He warns these few survivors not to go to Egypt, for it too would be invaded by Babylon and they would perish there. Sadly, they do not listen.

▸ **Chapters 46–51** *God's Judgment on the Nations*

In Jeremiah 25, Jeremiah proclaimed that all the nations around Judah are to "drink the cup" of God's wrath. Chapters 46–51 include a series of prophetic oracles against nine nations that faced God's judgment. These prophecies were probably given to Jeremiah at different times. They are now collected and recorded by nation: Egypt, Philistia, Moab, Ammon, Edom, Damascus (Syria), Arabia, Elam, and Babylonia.

▸ **Chapter 52** *God's Judgment on Jerusalem*

Jeremiah's 40 years of declaring doom culminates with the capture, destruction, and plunder of Jerusalem. The leaders are killed, and the survivors are taken to Babylon. This chapter is a review of the city's fall and a historical supplement to the account given in chapter 39. It confirms the accuracy of Jeremiah's prophecies concerning Jerusalem and Judah.

Putting Meat on the Bones

Most people's definitions of success would include the acquiring of wealth, popularity, fame, power, or accomplishments. By these standards, Jeremiah was a complete failure. For 40 years he served as God's spokesman and passionately urged the people to return to God, and no one listened, especially the kings. He was penniless, friendless, and rejected by his family. In the world's eyes, Jeremiah was not a success. But in God's eyes, Jeremiah was one of the most successful people in all biblical history. Why? Because success, as seen by God, involves obedience and faithfulness. Jeremiah obeyed God and, regardless of severe opposition and great personal sacrifice, committed himself to fulfilling God's calling on his life.

Fleshing It Out in Your Life

Acceptance or rejection by people is not to be the measure of your success. You must live a life that honors and glorifies God in spite of temptations and pressures that may lead you to do otherwise. God's approval alone should be the standard for your life and your service to Him.

Life Lessons from Jeremiah

- You must view success from God's perspective, not the world's.
- Commit yourself to being successful in God's eyes.
- Faithfulness to God requires your obedience, even when difficult decisions must be made.
- When the time arrives, God will give you the courage to speak up for your beliefs.
- Persecution and rejection are to be expected as you live a godly lifestyle.

Where to Find it

David's Branch . . . . Jeremiah 23:5-6
70 years of exile predicted . . . . Jeremiah 25:11-12
The time of Jacob's trouble . . . . Jeremiah 30:7
The New Covenant . . . . Jeremiah 31:31-33

The Response to Jeremiah's Ministry

Death threats	Isolation
Burning of the prophetic message	Imprisonment
Put in painful stocks	Rejection
Arrested	Starvation
Challenged by false prophets	Chains

God's Irrevocable Covenants

The Noahic Covenant—Genesis 9:8-17

The Abrahamic Covenant—Genesis 15:12-21

The Levitical Covenant—Numbers 25:10-13

The Davidic Covenant—2 Samuel 7:13; 23:5

The New Covenant—Jeremiah 31:31-34

Lamentations

My eyes fail with tears, my heart is troubled…
because of the destruction of my people.
(2:11)

Theme: Lament
Date written: 586 B.C.
Author: Jeremiah
Setting: Jerusalem

The book of Lamentations contains five poems that describe Jeremiah's eyewitness account of the destruction of Jerusalem by the Babylonian army. Jeremiah predicted this disaster in his earlier prophetic book, Jeremiah. Now he writes these five funeral poems to express his grief. But, as in his previous book, Jeremiah reminds readers that God has not and will not abandon His people. He is faithful, and His mercies continue to remain available to those who respond to His call.

The Skeleton

▸ **Chapter 1** *The First Lament: Jerusalem's Desolation*

In the first poem or lament, Jeremiah describes the city of Jerusalem as having been ruined by its enemies. The desolation, says the Lord, is not the result of bad luck or some accident. Rather, God sent punishment upon the people because they had abandoned His ways.

▸ **Chapter 2** *The Second Lament: God's Anger at Sin*

Jeremiah moves from the subject of Jerusalem's desolation to an eyewitness account of her destruction. God's anger over the people's sins is described, and this is followed by another round of heartfelt lament by Jeremiah.

▸ **Chapter 3** *The Third Lament: Hope in the Midst of Affliction*

Out of the depths of Jeremiah's grief comes a ray of hope. God's compassion is ever present and His faithfulness is great! Jeremiah realizes that it is only the mercy of God that has prevented total annihilation.

▸ **Chapter 4** *The Fourth Lament: God's Wrath Detailed*

The prophet rehearses the siege of Jerusalem and remembers the suffering and starvation of both the rich and the poor. He reviews the causes of the siege, especially the sins of Jerusalem's false prophets and priests. He closes this lament with a warning of punishment on the nation of Edom.

▸ **Chapter 5** *The Fifth Lament: A Prayer for Restoration*

Jeremiah concludes this sorrowful book with a prayer that God, in His mercy, will remember His people and restore and reestablish the kingdom in Israel.

Putting Meat on the Bones

There are three themes that run through the five laments of Jeremiah. The most apparent is the mourning over Jerusalem's destruction. In his sorrow, Jeremiah weeps for himself, for the suffering people, and sometimes for the city as if it were a person. The second theme is Jeremiah's confession of sin and acknowledgment of God's righteous and holy judgment of the nation. The third theme is the hope of God's promised future restoration of His people. God has poured out His wrath, but in His mercy, He will not cease to be faithful to His covenant promises.

Fleshing It Out in Your Life

Most of us don't like to show our emotions, especially our tears. But what makes a person cry says a lot about the person. In Jeremiah's case, the tears are for the suffering of God's people and their rebellion against their God. What causes you to cry? Do you weep because someone has insulted you or because someone has insulted God? Do you cry because you have lost something that gives you pleasure or because of the lostness of the people around you who will suffer eternally for their sinfulness? The world is filled with injustice, suffering, and rebellion against God, all of which should move you to tears and action.

Life Lessons from Lamentations

- The painful cry of lament over the misfortune and suffering of others is a valid form of prayer, one which God hears and answers.
- There are serious consequences when a nation—or a person—turns from God's ways.
- You can rest in the knowledge that God is faithful and merciful.
- Prayer is always appropriate in times of suffering.

Where to Find It

The announcement of Jerusalem's desolation . . . . Chapter 1
Jeremiah's lamentation over Israel's misery . . . . Chapter 2
A reminder of God's faithfulness and mercy . . . . Chapter 3
A description of the siege of Jerusalem . . . . Chapter 4
Jeremiah's plea for restoration . . . . Chapter 5

Jeremiah's Writings

The book of Jeremiah looks forward...	with warning.
The book of Lamentations looks backward...	with mourning.

Ezekiel

I arose and went out into the plain,
and behold, the glory of the LORD stood there,
like the glory which I saw by the River Chebar;
and I fell on my face.
(3:23)

Theme: The glory of the Lord
Date written: 590–570 B.C.
Author: Ezekiel
Setting: Babylon

While Jeremiah is prophesying in Jerusalem that the city would soon fall to the Babylonians, Ezekiel is giving a similar message to the captives who are already in Babylon. Like the people in Jerusalem, the captives could not believe that God would allow Jerusalem to be destroyed. After the news of the fall comes, Ezekiel changes his messages to one of future hope and restoration for the people. Throughout the book, Ezekiel describes his encounters with God's glory, whether it is His heavenly glory or His earthly glory in the temple of the past or the one predicted for the future.

The Skeleton

▸ Chapters 1–3 *The Call of Ezekiel*

The Babylonian conquest of Jerusalem takes place in stages, and the Jewish people are taken captive in three deportations (see page 60). Ezekiel, a priest, is taken to Babylon in the second deportation, in 597 B.C. While there, Ezekiel has a vision of God's heavenly glory. In the vision, God commissions Ezekiel to become a prophet to the Jewish people living in Babylon. Ezekiel is clearly warned by God that the people are rebellious and won't listen to his message.

▸ **Chapters 4–24** *The Judgment of Jerusalem*

God's judgment of the people of Judah and Jerusalem is already under way, with many Jewish people already taken captive in Babylon. Through Ezekiel, God continues to warn the people of Jerusalem's eventual collapse, and urges them to turn from their wicked ways. Ezekiel announces that God's glory will leave the temple, and that the temple will be destroyed.

▸ **Chapters 25–32** *The Judgment of the Nations*

After pronouncing judgment upon Jerusalem, Ezekiel goes on to pronounce God's retribution against several of the enemy nations surrounding Israel. These judgments affirm God's sovereign power over all kings and nations.

▸ **Chapters 33–39** *The Restoration of God's People*

Ezekiel announces the fall of Jerusalem and calls the Jewish people to repentance. Though the city and the temple are now in ruins, this is not the end. If the people are willing to turn from their rebellion against God, He will restore them and bring them back to their land.

▸ **Chapters 40–48** *The Restoration of Worship*

God gives Ezekiel a vision of Israel's spiritual future and a glorious new temple that will see the return of the glory of the Lord. God promises to restore the people and bring them back to Him.

Putting Meat on the Bones

Ezekiel places a strong emphasis on the sovereignty, glory, and faithfulness of God, and much of the book concentrates on the temple in Jerusalem with its perversion, destruction, and future restoration, as well as its connection to the glory of God. Throughout his messages, Ezekiel emphasizes again and again God's declaration that all the things to come are happening so that people "shall know that I am the Lord."

Everything that God does—past, present, or future, whether in grace or in judgment—is to reveal His glory.

Fleshing It Out in Your Life

God's glory is readily visible to anyone who is willing to look up at the heavens (Psalms 19:1). His glory is visible in His preservation of His covenant people and their promised restoration. It is visible in the plans He has made for His future temple and His coming kingdom. And it is visible in His grace toward repentant sinners during the church age. God is gloriously to be praised and worshipped. The very thought of His glory should drive you to make the changes in your life that help you to better reflect His holy nature.

Life Lessons from Ezekiel

- God normally does not use a person living in sin and rebellion. Through discipline, He can purge such a person, and call him to a new start.
- God disciplines when necessary, but He always leaves the door open for restoration.
- God has complete control over all people and all nations.
- God sovereignly controls every detail of your life, which should be a great comfort to you.

Where to Find It

The vision of God's glory . . . . Ezekiel 1:4-28
God's glory departs from the temple . . . . Ezekiel 11:22-25
The siege of Jerusalem begins . . . . Ezekiel 24:1-14
The watchman and his message . . . . Ezekiel 33:1-9
God's promise of a new heart . . . . Ezekiel 36:26-27
The valley of dry bones . . . . Ezekiel 37:1-14
God's glory returns to Jerusalem . . . . Ezekiel 43:1-9

How Ezekiel Acted Out His Prophecies

- He stayed in his house, tied up and mute.
- He used a clay tablet and iron plate.
- He lay on his left side for 390 days, and on his right side for 40 days.
- He ate in a unclean manner.
- He shaved his head and beard.
- He packed a bag and dug through a wall.
- He could not mourn when his wife died.
- He put two sticks together as one.

Daniel

The Most High God rules in the kingdom of men,
and appoints over it whomever He chooses.
(5:21)

Theme: The sovereignty of God
Date written: 530 B.C.
Author: Daniel
Setting: Babylon

The book of Daniel is called "the Apocalypse of the Old Testament." It is written to encourage the exiled Jews by revealing God's sovereign program for Israel during and after the period of Gentile domination. The "times of the Gentiles" (Luke 21:24) begins with the Babylonian captivity. The Jews will suffer under Gentile powers for a long time. But this period is not permanent, and a time will come when God will establish the Messianic kingdom, which will last forever. Daniel repeatedly emphasizes the sovereignty and power of God over human affairs. Because Daniel—"O man of high esteem"—is of such stellar character, God gives him a view of the future rivaled only by the apostle John's visions in the book of Revelation.

The Skeleton

▸ **Chapters 1–6** *Daniel's Life*

In the first of three deportations (see page 60), Daniel, thought by many to be a teenager at this time, is taken captive to Babylon along with other youths from Jerusalem, including his friends Shadrach, Meshach, and Abednego. King Nebuchadnezzar and the Babylonians want to train these four Jewish men to become part of their pagan culture. However, the four take a stand for righteousness in the face of great pressure, and take additional such stands as time goes on. God honors these young men for their boldness—for example, at one point Daniel is spared from a den of hungry lions, and on another occasion Daniel's friends are preserved from death in a fiery furnace. God also enables Daniel to interpret Nebuchadnezzar's dream of a statue that represents the four major earthly kingdoms that will rule the world until the time of Christ's return. Daniel's integrity and wisdom earns the respect of Nebuchadnezzar, who places Daniel in a high government office.

▸ **Chapters 7–12** *Daniel's Visions*

Daniel has four visions that look ahead into the future of Israel and the world. He proclaims the famous prophecy of the "seventy weeks," which includes mention of the seven years of tribulation that will mark the last days, and provides details about the identity of the Antichrist and the eventual restoration of Israel.

Putting Meat on the Bones

Daniel's life is rich in historical experiences and earthly honors. Carried captive to Babylon when he was a teen, Daniel spends his next 70-plus years in public service in a nation filled with idolatry and wickedness. In spite of his surroundings, Daniel lives a godly life and exercises tremendous influence in three kingdoms—Babylon, Media, and Persia. During these years, he could have despaired. He could have thought God had abandoned him. He could have cried, "Where is God?" Instead of giving in or giving up, this courageous man holds fast to his faith in God. Daniel understands that despite his circumstances, God is sovereign and is working out His plan for all nations, kings, and individuals.

Fleshing It Out in Your Life

Daniel and his three friends are inspiring examples of how to live a godly life in an ungodly world. Make sure your Christian distinctives don't get blurred through compromise with the world around you. Be faithful in your study of God's Word, sustain your prayer life, and maintain your integrity. Then, like Daniel, you will have a marked influence on those around you, starting with your family.

Life Lessons from Daniel

- God is sovereign over all history. Kingdoms rise and fall according to His plan.
- God honors you when you take a stand for what is right.
- God punishes sin.
- God already has a plan for the future, and because He is sovereign, it will come to pass.

Where to Find It

The fiery furnace .... Daniel 3
The handwriting on the wall .... Daniel 5
Daniel in the lions' den .... Daniel 6
Daniel's vision of the four beasts .... Daniel 7
Daniel's prophecy of the 70 weeks .... Daniel 9

The Four Kingdoms of Nebuchadnezzar's Statue

Body part	Material	Empire
Head	Gold	Babylonians
Chest and arms	Silver	Medo-Persians
Belly and thighs	Bronze	Greeks
Legs and feet	Iron and clay	Romans

The Kings Daniel Served

King Nebuchadnezzar of Babylonia	Chapters 1–4
Belshazzar of Babylonia	Chapter 5
Darius of Medo-Persia	Chapters 6–9
Durius of Medo-Persia	Chapters 10–12

Hosea

I will have mercy on her who had not obtained mercy; Then I will say to those who were not my people, "You are my people!" And they shall say, "You are my God!"
(2:23)

Theme: Unfaithfulness
Date written: 755–715 B.C.
Author: Hosea
Setting: Northern kingdom

Hosea is the next prophetic book, and it's the first of a series of 12 prophetic books called the Minor Prophets—not because they are less important, but because of their size. Each of the minor prophets is named after its author. Hosea's ministry begins during a time of prosperity in the northern kingdom. But the prosperity is only external. Inwardly, the people are idolatrous and wicked. In less than 30 years, Israel and its capital, Samaria, would fall.

The book of Hosea details the unhappy domestic union of a man and his unfaithful wife, Gomer. Their story serves as a vivid parallel of the loyalty of God and the spiritual adultery of Israel. With empathetic sorrow, Hosea, whose name means "salvation," exposes the sins of Israel and contrasts them to God's holiness. The nation must be judged for its sin, but it will be restored in the future because of the love and faithfulness of God. Hosea has been referred to as the prophet of restoration, and the book that bears his name depicts God's willingness to restore the unfaithful.

The Skeleton

▸ Chapters 1–3 *Israel's Adultery and God's Faithfulness*

God commands Hosea to marry Gomer and have children with her. She becomes unfaithful and commits adultery. Her unfaithfulness is representative of Israel's unfaithfulness to God. But just as Hosea shows patient love for Gomer, God still loves His people even in the midst of their immorality and rebellion. Hosea redeems his wife from the slave market and restores her to her position as his wife. In like fashion, idolatrous and unfaithful Israel will one day be completely restored in its relationship with God.

▸ Chapters 4–7 *Israel's Guilt*

Because of his painful experience with Gomer, Hosea can empathize with God's sorrow over the unfaithfulness of His people. Though Israel has hardened her heart to God's gracious last appeal to repent, even now there is still time for God to heal and redeem the people. However, they arrogantly continue in their rebellion.

▸ Chapters 8–10 *Israel's Indictment*

These chapters give the verdict of the case that Hosea has just presented for the sinfulness of Israel. The people's disobedience is about to lead them into exile and dispersion. Israel has spurned repentance, and the judgment of God can no longer be withheld. Hosea rebukes Israel for her moral depravity, apostasy, and idolatry.

▸ Chapters 11–14 *Israel's Salvation*

Hosea calls Israel to repentance and offers her a spiritual blessing for her return to faith. Though the people are now the recipients of a stern rebuke, the day is coming when they will receive a powerful blessing.

Putting Meat on the Bones

More than any other Old Testament prophet, Hosea's personal experience illustrates his prophetic message. He has a real compassion for God's people. Also, Hosea's personal suffering because of his wife's unfaithfulness gives him some understanding of God's grief over Israel's sin. Therefore Hosea's words of coming judgment are delivered with firmness yet tempered with a heart of affection. Hosea's tenderness illustrates God's faithfulness, justice, love, and forgiveness in contrast with Israel's corruption and apostasy. With great concern Hosea pleads on behalf of God for the people to return to God, but they will not.

Fleshing It Out in Your Life

Like Hosea, you too may experience times of emotional and physical suffering. However, rather than becoming bitter, you can allow God to use your suffering to comfort others in their pain. That's what was at the heart of Paul's message when he wrote, "If we are afflicted, it is for your consolation and salvation, which is effective for enduring the same sufferings which we also suffer" (2 Corinthians 1:6).

Life Lessons from Hosea

- God loves His people despite their sins and faults.
- You can count on God's faithfulness even when you are unfaithful.
- Repentance is the first step on the path back to relationship with God.
- God will give you the strength to resist the world's seduction.

Where to Find It

Gomer's marriage and children . . . . Chapter 1
Israel's leaders rebuked . . . . Chapter 5
A testimony of God's love . . . . Chapter 6
Israel's rebellion against God's love . . . . Chapter 11
Israel's future restoration and blessing . . . . Chapter 14

Chronological Order and Approximate Dates of the Minor Prophets

Obadiah	840 B.C.	Nahum	660 B.C.
Joel	835	Zephaniah	625
Jonah	760	Habakkuk	607
Amos	755	Haggai	520
Hosea	740	Zechariah	515
Micah	730	Malachi	430

Joel

Return to the LORD your God,
for He is gracious and merciful,
slow to anger, and of great kindness.
(2:13)

Theme: The day of the Lord
Date written: 835–796 B.C.
Author: Joel
Setting: Judah/Jerusalem

Because there are no specific events recorded in the book of Joel other than the invasion of locusts, it is difficult to determine when this book was written. Joel, however, appears to be one of the earlier prophets in Judah. He lived and ministered in Judah about the same time as Elisha and Jonah ministered in the northern kingdom of Israel. Joel predicts that the land will be invaded by a dreadful army that will make a recent locust invasion seem mild by comparison. On behalf of God, Joel appeals to the people to repent and avert the coming disaster.

The Skeleton

▸ **Chapter 1** *The Plague of Locusts*

Israel experiences a plague of locusts that brings desolation to the land. Joel explains that this is a foretaste of the coming "day of the LORD" (verse 15). In view of this catastrophe, Joel calls for humility and repentance.

▸ **Chapter 2** *The Day of the Lord*

Joel spells out the events of the coming day of judgment, when an army will invade from the north and a great struggle will occur. For those who repent, it is promised that the Spirit of God will be poured out.

▸ **Chapter 3** *Judgment and Blessing*

The Lord will judge the nations, especially those which have mistreated His chosen people. Israel will receive a special blessing and be revived and restored.

Putting Meat on the Bones

A single bomb can destroy a large city. A single earthquake or hurricane can destroy whole civilizations. We stand in awe at the power and might of both natural and man-made power. But these forces cannot touch the power of Almighty God. Ever since the first sin was committed in the Garden of Eden in Genesis, man has been in rebellion against God. Judah has now taken its turn in disregarding God's laws. Because the people do not repent, they will surely have their day of judgment, their "day of the LORD." Rebellion continues to be allowed by God, but a future day is coming when all rebellion will be punished.

Fleshing It Out in Your Life

God—not foreign invaders, nature, or the economy—is the one with whom all must reckon. One cannot ignore or offend God forever. You must pay attention to His message from His Word. If you don't, you will face "the day of the LORD" later. Where do you stand with God and His coming judgment? Where does Joel's message find you today? It's not too late to ask for and receive God's forgiveness. God's greatest desire is for you to come to Him.

Life Lessons from Joel

- God always gives a warning before He sends judgment.
- God brings judgment if there is no repentance.

- Humility and repentance are necessary to restore your relationship with God.
- Sin brings God's day of reckoning.

Where to Find It

Judah's invasion and destruction by locusts . . . . .Chapter 1
Judah's desolation by Assyria . . . . .Chapter 2
Judah and Israel's restoration by God . . . . .Chapter 3

"The day of the Lord"
is mentioned
19 times in the Old Testament
(5 times in Joel)
4 times in the New Testament.

Amos

Seek good and not evil, that you may live;
so the LORD God of hosts
will be with you....
(5:14)

Theme: Punishment
Date written: 790 B.C.
Author: Amos
Setting: Bethel, the northern kingdom

Amos is a shepherd and a cultivator of sycamore trees from a rural area south of Jerusalem. He is gripped by God and divinely commissioned to leave his homeland and preach a harsh message of judgment to the northern kingdom of Israel. He offers eight pronouncements—three sermons and five visions—warning of coming disaster because of complacency, idolatry, and the oppression of the poor. But because of the peace and prosperity of Israel during this period, his message falls on deaf ears.

The Skeleton

▸ **Chapters 1–2** *Pronouncement of Judgment*

The prophet Amos names specific sins of various nations and pronounces eight judgments upon the nations. Then Amos describes the transgressions of the people of Israel and Judah and warns of future destruction and condemnation from the Lord. Among the sins of the nations and the Jewish people is idolatry—the worship of false gods.

▸ Chapters 3–6 *Reasons for Judgment*

In these chapters, Amos delivers three sermons exposing Israel's sin. Among the problems in Israel are greed, excessive taxation, and cruel oppression of the poor. God condemns those who "crush the needy" (4:1), take bribes, and deprive the poor of justice (5:12). Though the people profess to follow God and offer sacrifices to Him, their hypocrisy is evident in their excessive lifestyle. There is a total absence of social justice and morality.

▸ Chapters 7–9 *Visions of Judgment and Restoration*

Amos has five visions that depict what God will do to punish Israel. Yet in spite of all the people have done wrong, God still loves them and promises there will come a future day of restoration and blessing.

Putting Meat on the Bones

Amos is not a professional prophet. He has not been to "prophet school." He says, "I was no prophet, nor was I a son of a prophet, but I was a sheepbreeder and a tender of sycamore fruit" (7:14). He is a simple country boy. What is it then that makes him such a powerful spiritual force? In his testimony he gives us the answer: "Then the LORD took me...and the Lord said to me, 'Go, prophesy to My people Israel'" (verse 15). Amos fearlessly prophesied by the Spirit of God within him (3:8).

Fleshing It Out in Your Life

Amos provides an excellent example for you today. He reminds you that you don't have to be professionally trained to speak up for God when you see human injustice or sinful behavior, especially by those who claim to be Christians. Amos was a fiery spokesman for God not because of education or birth, but because he was obedient when the call of God came. You too can be God's person. Listen for His call and do what He asks. Then watch as the power of God works through you as you serve Him.

Life Lessons from Amos

- God cares about the poor and those in need, and so should you.
- Whenever you have the opportunity to show compassion, you should act upon it.
- It is wrong to enrich yourself at the expense of others.
- If your heart is far from God and you are living in disobedience, then your words and actions mean nothing.
- Complacency happens almost without notice. Check and renew your heart daily.
- Judgment is certain for those who ignore God.

Where to Find It

Prophecy of Israel's coming destruction . . . . Chapter 3
Israel's reproof and disregard . . . . Chapter 4
Amos's call to repentance . . . . Chapter 5
Scattering and restoration of Israel . . . . Chapter 9

The Five Visions of Amos

1. Vision of the locusts (7:1-3)
2. Vision of the fire (7:4-6)
3. Vision of the plumb line (7:7-9)
4. Vision of the summer fruit (8:1-14)
5. Vision of the Lord (9:1-10)

Obadiah

No survivor shall remain of the house of Esau.
(Verse 18)

Theme: Righteous judgment
Time: 850–840 B.C.
Author: Obadiah
Setting: Jerusalem/Edom

Obadiah, the shortest Old Testament book—one chapter long—and possibly the earliest of the prophetic books, is a dramatic example of God's response to anyone who would harm His chosen people. Edom was a mountainous nation to the southeast of Israel. As descendants of Esau (Genesis 25–27), the Edomites are blood relatives of the people of Judah. And, of all people, they should rush to the aid of Judah when it was under attack. Instead, the Edomites gloat over Judah's problems. They capture and deliver survivors to the enemy, and even loot Judah's land. Because of Edom's indifference, defiance of God, and treachery toward their brothers in Judah, Obadiah gives them God's message of coming disaster.

The Skeleton

▸ **Verses 1–16** *Edom's Destruction*

The people of Edom feel secure because their capital city, Petra, is hidden among high peaks that make the city easy to protect. The people of Edom are filled with pride and self-confidence. Their arrogance is evident in verse 3 as they marvel, "Who will bring me down to the ground?" When Jerusalem is attacked by an unnamed enemy, the Edomites do not come to help the people of Jerusalem, but instead encourage the attackers, help take some of the people captive, and even plunder the city. This angers God, who promises the Edomites that "though you ascend as high as the eagle, and though you set your nest among the stars, from there I will bring you down" (verse 4).

▸ **Verses 17–21** *Israel's Restoration*

Those who take pride in their power and defy the Lord will face judgment. God promises to completely destroy the Edomites and to restore His people to a place of prominence.

Putting Meat on the Bones

Bible scholars aren't sure about which invasion of Judah Obadiah refers to in his book, but the message is clear: God judges those who harm His children or aid in their harm. This was true of Edom in the past, and it will be true of any nation in the future.

Fleshing It Out in Your Life

On a more positive and personal note, if you are a child of God through Jesus Christ, you are under His love and protection. Nothing will befall you that isn't under God's directive hand. Ultimately judgment will fall on all who harm His chosen people, Israel, or His adopted people, believers in Jesus Christ.

Life Lessons from Obadiah

- Those who persecuted God's people in the Bible were always brought to justice. Likewise, those who are hostile to Christians today can expect to face God's judgment.
- When you see harm being inflicted upon fellow Christians, you should not worsen the situation by abandoning them, but rather, come to their aid.
- Take no pleasure in the misfortune of others.
- Pride and self-centeredness will reap destruction.

Where to Find It

Edom's destruction . . . . Verses 1-16
Israel's restoration . . . . Verses 17-21

The History of the Conflict Between Israel and Edom

- Israel descended from Jacob, and Edom from Esau.
- Jacob and Esau struggled in their mother's womb.
- Esau sold his birthright to Jacob.
- The Edomites refused to let the Israelites pass through their land after the Exodus.
- Israel's kings faced constant conflict with Edom.
- Edom urged Babylon to destroy Jerusalem.

Jonah

I know that You are a gracious and merciful God,
slow to anger and abundant in lovingkindness,
One who relents from doing harm.
(4:2)

Theme: God's grace to all people
Date written: 780–750 B.C.
Author: Jonah
Setting: Nineveh

Jonah is the autobiography of a reluctant prophet who did not want to preach repentance to Israel's enemy, the godless Assyrians, and their capital city, Nineveh. The book is unusual because it is the only Old Testament book whose exclusive message is to a Gentile nation. God's declaration is that His grace is extended to the Gentiles as well as to His covenant people, Israel. Jonah's message was received with an almost immediate response of repentance exhibited by fasting and mournful behavior. As a result, the city of 600,000 people is spared.

The Skeleton

▸ Chapters 1–2 *Jonah's Call and Disobedience*

God calls Jonah, a resident in the northern kingdom, to go preach repentance in Nineveh, the greatest and most powerful city-state of its time. In his patriotic zeal, Jonah puts his country before his God. Rebelling against his commission from God, Jonah catches a ship to escape his mission. Instead of going 500 miles northeast to Nineveh, Jonah attempts to go 2000 miles west to Tarshish (Spain). The ship is caught in a devastating storm, and Jonah is cast into the sea by those on board hoping to escape the wrath of the storm caused by Jonah's presence and disobedience. Jonah is then swallowed by a great fish. God uses the fish to rescue Jonah, get his attention, and finally deposit him on dry land.

▸ **Chapters 3–4** *Jonah's Renewed Call*

Jonah, in obedience to God's second call, preaches to the inhabitants of Nineveh. They repent, mourning their sin, and God spares the city. However, Jonah is angered that God has shown His mercy to these pagans. God then lets Jonah know that He intends to offer His grace and mercy to all people.

Putting Meat on the Bones

How would you react if you were asked by God to take the gospel message to your country's worst enemy? You now know what Jonah's reaction was. In his heart he knew that no one deserved judgment more than the Assyrians. They were a godless and wickedly cruel people, and Jonah desired their destruction. Eventually, however, with God's helping hand, Jonah does go and preach his one-line message: "Yet forty days, and Nineveh shall be overthrown!" (3:4). And, much to Jonah's displeasure, the people respond! Then God confronts Jonah's self-righteousness and lack of compassion.

Fleshing It Out in Your Life

Have you ever been like Jonah? Do you sometimes flee from opportunities to share the truth of your Savior with those around you? Do you move around with heartless indifference, saying nothing about God's saving grace to workmates, neighbors, friends, and family? Don't follow Jonah's example. Instead, follow God's example and develop a genuine love and compassion for the lost. Begin praying for those who seem to be the farthest from God. Then look for ways to share "the good news" with them. Who knows, maybe they too will respond to God's message and repent! Pray that they do.

Life Lessons from Jonah

- You cannot escape God's call on your life. He will pursue you to the ends of the earth…or as in Jonah's case, into the belly of a big fish!
- God's love and mercy are for all people.
- Disobedience leads to catastrophe in your life.
- It is impossible to run away from God.
- There is no limit to what God will—and can!—use to get your attention.
- Failure does not necessarily disqualify you from God's service.
- Your disobedience affects the lives of others you come in contact with.
- Nationalism/patriotism should never stand in the way of God's plan.

Where to Find It

F leeing from God's presence . . . . Chapter 1
I n the belly of the great fish . . . . Chapter 2
S peaking God's truth in Nineveh . . . . Chapter 3
H oping for Nineveh's destruction . . . . Chapter 4

Jonah's Journey to Nineveh

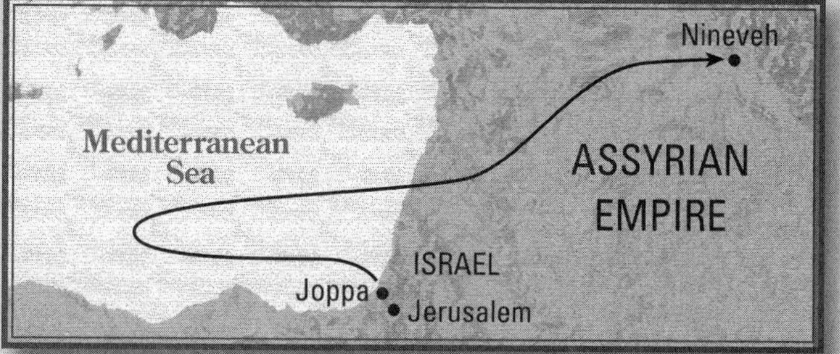

God commanded Jonah to go to Nineveh, but Jonah did not want to go, for the people of the Assyrian Empire were very wicked. Jonah tried to go in the opposite direction by taking a ship to Tarshish. God intervened, and pointed Jonah back toward Nineveh.

Micah

He has shown you, O man, what is good;
and what does the Lord *require of you but to do justly,*
to love mercy, and to walk humbly with your God?
(6:8)

Theme: Divine judgment
Date written: 735–710 B.C.
Author: Micah
Setting: Samaria and Jerusalem

Micah, in similar fashion to other prophets such as Hosea and Amos, proclaims a message of judgment to a people persistently pursuing evil. He presents his three oracles, or cycles, of doom and hope as if he were in a courtroom. Each message presented (mainly to the southern kingdom of Judah, but also to the northern kingdom) begins with the admonition to "hear." The book begins with judgment for Israel's unfaithfulness, and ends on a strong note that the Lord intends to fulfill the unconditional promises He made to Abraham and Jacob in regard to Israel.

The Skeleton

▸ **Chapters 1–2** *The Trial of the Capitals*

"Hear all you peoples." Micah summons all the nations into "court" to hear testimony against Samaria and Jerusalem, the capitals of the northern and southern kingdoms, regarding their oppression of the poor, the hypocrisy of the national and religious leaders, and the errant words of false prophets. God's people are not living according to God's plan.

▸ **Chapters 3–5** *The Trial of the Leaders*

"Hear now, O heads of Jacob." Micah first addresses Israel's corrupt rulers, who should be aware of injustice. Yet their conduct toward the poor is likened to the butchering of animals. But Micah also gives a prophetic glimpse of the glorious future, speaking of a "Messianic kingdom" that will be established when the Lord regathers His people. This kingdom will be established by the coming Messiah, Jesus Christ, who will avenge all wrongs and bring spiritual blessing.

▸ **Chapters 6–7** *The Trial of the People*

"Hear, O you mountains, the LORD's complaint." Micah rebukes God's people for their ingratitude and for forsaking the practices God had given them. He also reminds them that confession and repentance will lead to a fulfillment of all God's promises.

Putting Meat on the Bones

Like the prophet Amos, Micah is a country boy. Unlike the prophet Isaiah, who at this same time is at the king's court in Jerusalem and aware of the *political conditions of the region*, Micah shows a profound concern for the *sufferings of the common people.* Micah champions the cause of the poor as he warns the leaders of the consequences of their exploitation. Because of corruption among the wealthy, Micah's message of imminent judgment is not popular. Micah's concern can be summarized in what God wants to see in His people: Justice and equity tempered with mercy and compassion as the result of a humble and obedient relationship with the Lord (6:8).

Fleshing It Out in Your Life

Micah emphasizes the inherent relationship between true spirituality and social ethics. Or, as James describes it in the New Testament, the relationship between faith and works. True faith in God generates kindness, compassion, justice, and humility. You can please God by living above reproach and nurturing these qualities in your relationships at work, at church, with your neighbors, and with your family.

Life Lessons from Micah

- God condemns those who oppress and take advantage of the poor.
- True religion should result in righteous acts.
- God requires not only personal righteousness but also social responsibility.
- Your religion cannot be divorced from your relationships.

Where to Find It

The trial of Jerusalem and Samaria	Chapter 1
The reasons for judgment	Chapter 2
The trial of Israel's leaders	Chapter 3
The prophecies of a future kingdom	Chapter 4
The prophecy of a Messiah from Bethlehem	Chapter 5
The trial of the people	Chapter 6
God's promise of forgiveness and restoration	Chapter 7

God's List of Injustices Committed by the Leaders and the People

Devising iniquity and evil	Micah 2:1
Coveting, oppression, and violence	Micah 2:2
Stealing and dishonesty	Micah 2:8
Casting out of widows	Micah 2:9
Hating good and loving evil	Micah 3:1-2
Abhorring justice and perverting fairness	Micah 3:9
Shedding blood	Micah 3:10
Taking bribes	Micah 3:11

Nahum

The LORD is slow to anger and great in power,
and will not at all acquit the wicked.
(1:3)

Theme: Consolation
Date written: 690–640 B.C.
Author: Nahum
Setting: Jerusalem and Nineveh

About 100 years earlier, the prophet Jonah had visited Nineveh and warned of God's coming judgment. The people listened and repented, and God spared the city. But with the passage of time, Nineveh once again becomes a wicked city marked by murder, cruelty, idolatry, and social injustice. Nineveh is the capital of the Assyrian Empire, now the most powerful nation in the world and seemingly the most invincible. But no one can stand against God, who is sovereign over all the earth. According to Nahum, because of Nineveh's sins, this proud, powerful nation will be utterly destroyed. The end would come within 50 years.

The Skeleton

▸ Chapter 1 *The Promise of Nineveh's Destruction*

Nahum begins with a very clear description of the character of the Lord. He is righteous and just. He is patient and powerful. He is gracious to all who respond to Him, but overthrows all who rebel against Him. God is holy, and Nineveh stands condemned because of its sin.

▸ **Chapter 2** *The Details of Nineveh's Destruction*

Nahum describes how the destruction will take place. Attackers (the Medes and Babylonians) will come and cause great confusion in the city. The people will attempt to flee and will be taken captive. The city will be plundered of all its wealth. God promises the destruction will be complete. Assyria will be utterly destroyed never to return, but Judah will be restored.

▸ **Chapter 3** *The Reasons for Nineveh's Destruction*

In a series of accusations, Nahum explains the reasons for God's punishment of Nineveh. The fact that the people of the city are so wicked reveals God's judgment to be deserved.

Putting Meat on the Bones

Nahum portrays the patience, power, holiness, and justice of the living God. He may be slow to express His wrath, but His righteous vengeance is certain. This book gives the kingdom of Judah some rays of hope. Even though Judah, along with all the nations surrounding her, has been swallowed up by Assyria, the people in Judah who trust in the Lord can be consoled to hear of God's coming judgment upon the proud and brutal Assyrians.

Fleshing It Out in Your Life

The book and message of Nahum can also give you great consolation for the uncertain times in which you live today. You must constantly remember God's character and nature, and not be afraid of any power or people. God is in control of all events and is able to protect and provide for His children.

Life Lessons from Nahum

- Even the most powerful enemies who threaten or oppress God's people will one day fall. No one can hide from God's judgment.

- God not only holds individuals responsible for their actions, but whole cities and nations, too.
- The same God who hated evil in Bible times still hates evil today.

Where to Find It

GOD...		NINEVEH...
	Chapter 1	
is patient, powerful, and holy		is evil, corrupt, and judged
	Chapter 2	
punishes Nineveh		is destroyed
	Chapter 3	
details Nineveh's destruction		is utterly ruined

Another Message of Consolation

Do not be deceived, God is not mocked;
for whatever a man sows, that he will also reap.
For he who sows to his flesh
will of the flesh reap corruption,
but he who sows to the Spirit
will of the Spirit reap everlasting life.

(Galatians 6:7-8)

Habakkuk

The just shall live by his faith.
(2:4)

♳

Theme: Trusting a sovereign God
Date written: 607 B.C.
Author: Habakkuk
Setting: Judah

Toward the end of the kingdom of Judah, things had gone from bad to worse. Good King Josiah had been killed in battle, and all the reforms he put into place during his reign were quickly perverted by a rapid succession of bad kings—three sons and a grandson. This unchecked wickedness causes Habakkuk, a little-known prophet and a contemporary of Jeremiah, to question God's silence and apparent lack of judgment in purging His covenant people. Like Job, Habakkuk asks, "Why?" The second time the prophet asks this, God answers with a torrent of proof and predictions. Habakkuk finally catches a glimpse of the character and nature of God, and in response, can only stand back in awe and praise of Him.

The Skeleton

▸ **Chapters 1–2** *Habakkuk's Problem*

Habakkuk has a problem with understanding God's ways: "Why, God, are you allowing the wicked in Judah to go unpunished?" God gives an answer the prophet doesn't expect: God will use the Babylonians to punish Judah.

Now Habakkuk has an even bigger problem: "How can you, the

righteous Judge, punish Judah through a nation that is even more wicked?" God answers back that He is aware of Babylon's sin, and assures that the Babylonians will not escape His terrible judgment. But Judah, says God, is guilty of similar offenses and stands under the same condemnation.

The Lord concludes His answer to Habakkuk with a statement affirming His sovereign majesty: The LORD is in His holy temple, let all the earth keep silence before Him" (2:20).

▸ **Chapter 3** *Habakkuk's Prayer and Song of Praise*

The prophet began this short book by questioning God, but now concludes with a psalm or song of praise. He understands and acknowledges God's wisdom at the coming invasion by the Babylonians. The thought of judgment from an evil nation terrifies him, but he will trust God. And why not? God's faithful, creative, and redemptive work on the part of the Jewish people should give the prophet confidence in the divine purposes and continued hope even now, even when he would otherwise despair.

Putting Meat on the Bones

Habakkuk is what many people today would term a "free spirit." He liked to venture "outside the box" and wrestle with issues that tested his faith. He looked around and saw the people of Judah in blatant sin with no restraints. Injustice was widespread. Habakkuk openly and honestly directs his concerns to God and waits to see how God responds to his probing questions. God says He will judge the people of Judah, and to Habakkuk's surprise, God says He will use wicked Babylon as His instrument of justice.

Fleshing It Out in Your Own Life

The core of Habakkuk's message resides in the call to trust God—"The just shall live by his faith" (2:4). God is at work in the lives of His people even when it seems evil has triumphed. Because God is righteous and sovereign, He will not let injustice continue forever. At times, you may think that God's ways seem incomprehensible, but just as He was in control in Habakkuk's day, He is still in control today. Your responsibility is to not question God's actions or what seems like a lack of action. Your responsibility is to gain a better understanding of God's character. A true believer—one declared righteous by God—will steadfastly persevere in faith in spite of what is happening to him or to others. He understands and trusts the sovereign God who does only that which is right.

Life Lessons from Habakkuk

- Faith is not a one-time act. It's a way of life.
- You are called to trust God...even when life seems impossible and incomprehensible.
- The wicked may appear to be victorious, but ultimately our righteous God will punish them.
- God's ways are not our ways. They are beyond our understanding.

Where to Find It

Habakkuk questions God .... Chapter 1
"Why do the wicked go unpunished?"

God answers Habakkuk .... Chapter 2
"Judgment, though slow, will surely come."

Habakkuk prays to God .... Chapter 3
"O LORD, I have heard Your speech and was afraid; O LORD revive Your work in the midst of the years! In the midst of the years make it known; in wrath remember mercy" (3:2).

The next time you are troubled, remember to...

- Bring your problem directly to God—Habakkuk prayed.
- Believe and trust in God—Habakkuk responded in faith.
- Be encouraged—Habakkuk went from doubt to faith.
- Be sure to realize the problem is never with God—Habakkuk's problem was a limited understanding of God's ways.

Zephaniah

Seek the LORD, all you meek of the earth,
who have upheld His justice.
Seek righteousness, seek humility.
It may be that you will be hidden
in the day of the LORD'S anger.
(2:3)

Theme: The "great day of the LORD"
Date written: 635–625 B.C.
Author: Zephaniah
Setting: Jerusalem

Zephaniah is a great-great-grandson of the godly King Hezekiah. Because of his royal heritage, Zephaniah probably has free access to the court of King Josiah, during whose reign he prophesies. His preaching ministry may have played a significant role in preparing Judah for the revival that comes with this last good king of Judah. Zephaniah's message warns of the coming "great day of the LORD" (1:14), a day of judgment, first upon Judah and then upon the Gentile nations. As in the other prophetic books, God also promises to restore the fortunes of His people.

The Skeleton

▸ **Chapters 1–3:8** *The Lord's Judgment*

Zephaniah begins his prophetic ministry with an awesome statement about God's coming judgment upon the entire earth on account of sin. Then Zephaniah zeros in on the immediate judgment of Judah, listing some of the offenses of which she is guilty. Then he pronounces judgment on the nations all around Judah. Finally, the prophet comes back to Jerusalem and characterizes her as living in spiritual rebellion and moral depravity.

▸ **Chapter 3:9-20** *The Lord's Deliverance*

After spending most of his message speaking of God's judgment, Zephaniah changes his tone and proclaims God's future blessing, for this too is an aspect of the day of the Lord. There is coming a day when the nations will be purified and the Gentiles will call on the name of the Lord. A remnant of the nation of Israel will be regathered, redeemed, and restored. The multitudes will rejoice in their Savior, and He will be in their midst. What starts out in Zephaniah 3:9 as a small chorus gains momentum and swells into a crescendo that lists the many blessings God will bestow on His redeemed.

Putting Meat on the Bones

Zephaniah is another of the eleventh-hour prophets in the last days of Judah, with Jeremiah and Habakkuk being the others. The reforms in Zephaniah's day were too little and too late. Wickedness is so ingrained in the people that soon after the death of good King Josiah, they revert back to idolatry. Zephaniah prophesied that this would happen and that the judgment called "the day of the LORD" would come. This book expands on the similar theme of "the day of the LORD" in the book of Joel. Using varied terms, Zephaniah refers to the day of the Lord 23 times in the three chapters of his book. This day of the Lord would come soon upon Judah, but it would also have a future fulfillment. Jesus alluded to Zephaniah's day of the Lord in Matthew 13:41-43 and 24:29-31, and on both occasions He associated it with His second coming. The first day of the Lord refers to Judah's imminent devastation, which is only a prelude to the day when Jesus Christ will come to judge all of creation, all sin, and all the nations of the world. But as promised elsewhere, God will regather and restore His people, and there will come a day of worldwide rejoicing.

Fleshing It Out in Your Life

The message is clear for you today. If you acknowledge Jesus as

Lord, you, along with the righteous remnant of Israel, will escape the coming day of the Lord and one day enter into His blessed kingdom. The rejoicing that will come on that wonderful day when God has completely exerted His rulership can become yours today as you put your faith and trust in Jesus, the coming Messiah.

Life Lessons from Zephaniah

- No matter how difficult life is now, you can look forward to a day of rejoicing, a day when God will restore all things to what they should be.
- Don't let material comfort become a barrier to your commitment to God.
- Spiritual complacency will have its consequences.
- You can always find hope in the truth that our God reigns, and that He will take care of His own.

Where to Find It

The fact of Judah's coming day of judgment . . . . Chapter 1
The call to repentance . . . . Chapter 2
The coming of wrath and restoration . . . . Chapter 3

~ The Day of the Lord ~
Two Fulfillments

NEAR	*FAR*
Obadiah 1-14	Obadiah 15-21
Joel 1:15; 2:1,11	Joel 2:31; 3:14
Amos 5:18-20	———
———	Isaiah 2:12
Isaiah 13:6	Isaiah 13:9
Ezekiel 13:5; 30:3	———
———	Zechariah 14:1
———	Malachi 4:5

Haggai

Now therefore, thus says the LORD of hosts:
"Consider your ways!"
(1:5)

Theme: Rebuilding the temple
Date written: 520 B.C.
Author: Haggai
Setting: Judah

Haggai opens the last section of the Minor Prophets. He is one of three prophets preaching to the Jewish people who had returned from exile, Zechariah and Malachi being the other two. Prophets of the past had to deal with idolatry. But 70 years of exile had cured the people of this evil. Haggai's message is different. He urges God's people to stop thinking about their own comforts. Instead, they were to put their energies into the restoration of the temple. Build the house of God!

Amazingly, after having rejected the prophetic messages of the past, the people now listen to Haggai. Their hearts are stirred, and they take up the work of rebuilding the temple. God then honors the people's reshaped priorities and blesses their personal lives.

The Skeleton

▸ **Chapter 1** *A Call to Completion*

Discouraged by the opposition from their neighbors, the Jewish people have become indifferent to rebuilding the temple. Instead, they have put their energies into rebuilding their own homes and fortunes. Through Haggai, God urges them to consider carefully the consequences of their misplaced priorities. Haggai points out that the people's selfish concerns have caused many economic hardships, including the fact God has withheld rain for their crops. The people and leaders take Haggai's message to heart. Only 23 days after his first message, the people "obeyed the voice of the LORD" and "feared the presence of the LORD." They begin working again on the temple after 16 years of inactivity, and finish it four years later.

▸ **Chapter 2:1-9** *A Call to Courage*

About a month after the rebuilding starts up, the people, especially the elderly, become discouraged. Many of them remembered Solomon's temple, a far more glorious structure. This new temple wasn't as elegant. But the Lord urges the people to persevere and be courageous, assuring them of His presence and His faithfulness to fulfill His promises, which includes a greater, more glorious temple in the future.

▸ **Chapter 2:10-19** *A Call to Cleansing*

Two months after the exhortation that the people keep up their courage, God uses the priests and the ceremonial law as an object lesson to further motivate the people to continue working on the temple. The message is that if a holy sacrifice can become defiled, so will an offering to God be unacceptable as long as the people neglect the rebuilding of the temple.

▸ **Chapter 2:20-23** *A Call to the Chosen One*

On the same day that Haggai addresses the priests, he gives a second prophetic message to Zerubbabel, the leader of the exiles and a descendant of David. Using a distinctly Messianic title pointing to Christ, God calls Zerubbabel "My servant" and says He will make Zerubbabel like a "signet ring," which is a symbol of honor, authority, and power.

Putting Meat on the Bones

After 70 years of exile, God's people are being allowed to return to their homeland. Upon arrival, their first order of business is to rebuild the temple. But opposition from their Gentile neighbors and indifference from their own people cause the work to be abandoned. Now, 16 years later, God commissions Haggai, along with Zechariah, to stir up the people to not only rebuild the temple, but to order anew their spiritual priorities. During those 16 years the people had focused on themselves and allowed God's temple to lay in ruins. Haggai explains to the people that this lack of commitment to God's priorities is the reason they lack God's blessings.

Fleshing It Out in Your Life

Haggai's message to God's people applies very much to you today. What are your priorities? Take a good look at your checkbook. It will tell a fairly accurate story of where you have placed your priorities. Haggai asks you the same question he asked the people, "Are you building your own house and allowing God's house and God's ministries to go neglected?"

Life Lessons from Haggai

- God rewards those who put Him first and seek to do His will.
- You cannot dwell on the glory of the past. Reality is in the present.
- Review your priorities often. Are they in line with God's?
- Your service to God is vitally important.

Where to Find It

The command to build God's house . . . . Chapter 1
The encouragement to complete God's house . . . . Chapter 2

Places of Worship in the Bible

TYPE	*EXAMPLE and/or REFERENCE*
Altars	Abraham, Genesis 12:7-8
Tabernacle of God	
Built	Exodus 25–27; 36–39; 40
Set up in Shiloh	Joshua 18:1
Set up in Gibeon	2 Chronicles 1:2-5
Solomon's temple	1 Kings 6
Zerubbabel's temple	Haggai 1:1,14; 2:1; Zechariah 4:9
Zerubbabel's temple further rebuilt by Herod	Matthew 4:5; 21:12
The future millennial temple	Ezekiel 40–44

Zecharia h

I will return to Zion, and
dwell in the midst of Jerusalem.
Jerusalem shall be called the City of Truth,
The Mountain of the Lord of hosts,
the Holy Mountain.
(8:3)

Theme: God's deliverance
Date written: 520–480 B.C.
Author: Zechariah
Setting: Jerusalem

Zechariah, like Ezekiel and Jeremiah, is a priest as well as a prophet. Zechariah's prophetic ministry overlaps that of his older contemporary, Haggai, and imparts a series of eight visions, four messages, and two burdensome oracles over a two-year period. The first eight chapters of Zechariah are written to encourage the remnant while they were rebuilding the temple. The last six chapters are written sometime after the completion of the temple in anticipation of Israel's coming Messiah. This book is second only to Isaiah in the volume of material about the Messiah, the Lord Jesus Christ.

The Skeleton

▸ **Chapters 1–6** *Eight Night Visions*

In these chapters, Zechariah shares these eight night visions:

- A man among the myrtle trees—God will rebuild Zion

- Four horns and four craftsmen—Israel's oppressors will be judged
- The man with the measuring line—God will protect Jerusalem
- The cleansing of Joshua the high priest—Israel will be cleansed by the Messiah
- The golden lampstand—God's Spirit is empowering Zerubbabel and Joshua
- The flying scroll—individual sin will be judged
- The woman in a basket—the nation's sin will be removed
- The four chariots—God's judgment will come upon the nations

There is an interlude during which Zechariah records the coronation of Joshua as the high priest and the anticipation of the coming of the "Branch" who will be both King and Priest (Jesus Christ).

▸ **Chapters 7–8** *Four Messages*

In response to a question from some of the leaders about the continuation of the fasts, God gives Zechariah a series of four messages, which focus on these themes:

- A rebuke for wrong motives associated with fasting
- A call for the people to remember the consequence of their disobedience—destruction
- A promise of the future restoration of Zion, when God will dwell in Jerusalem
- An announcement that fasting would one day cease and be replaced by joyous feasts celebrating God's blessings

▸ **Chapters 9–14** *Two Burdensome Messages*

- The first message concerns the Messiah's (or Christ's) first coming and rejection.
- The second message concerns the Messiah's second coming and acceptance. He will come and cleanse the people of their impurities and falsehoods and will judge the nations and reign over the whole earth from Jerusalem.

Putting Meat on the Bones

Zechariah is an important prophetic book that gives detailed messianic references that are clearly fulfilled in the life of Jesus Christ. The rebuilding of the temple, Zechariah says, is only a first act in the drama of God's history.

Fleshing It Out in Your Life

God keeps His promises. Jesus, the promised Messiah and great deliverer of Israel, did come. He came first as the suffering Savior predicted by Isaiah. But He is also coming as the Judge and King who will reign forever and ever. The future is certain. Deliverance is coming. Your future can be certain, too, if you trust in Jesus, who is coming again.

Life Lessons from Zechariah

- The future holds no fear when Jesus is your Savior.
- God never fails to keep His promises.
- God's message of the coming Messiah should motivate your present and inspire your future.

Where to Find It

Prediction of Jesus riding a donkey . . . . Zechariah 9:9

Prediction of Jesus' betrayal for 30 shekels of silver . . . . Zechariah 11:4-13

Prediction of Jesus' return to the Mount of Olives . . . . Zechariah 14:4

Prophecies of Christ's Comings

Christ's First Coming:	Zechariah 3:8
	Zechariah 9:9,16
	Zechariah 11:11-13
Christ's Second Coming:	Zechariah 6:12
	Zechariah 12:10
	Zechariah 13:1,6
	Zechariah 14:1-21

Feasts in the Bible

THE FEAST	*THE FULFILLMENT IN CHRIST*
The Feast of Passover	Fulfilled in Christ's death
The Feast of Atonement	Fulfilled in the acceptance of Christ's salvation
The Feast of First Fruits	Fulfilled in Christ's resurrection
The Feast of Pentecost	Fulfilled in the arrival of the Holy Spirit
The Feast of Tabernacles	Is still appropriate to observe during Christ's reign

Malachi

"Bring all the tithes into the storehouse, that there may be food in My house, and try me now in this," says the LORD of hosts, "if I will not open for you the windows of heaven and pour out for you such blessing that there will not be room enough to receive it."
(3:10)

♁

Theme: Formalism rebuked
Date: About 430 B.C.
Author: Malachi
Setting: Jerusalem

Malachi is probably a contemporary of Ezra and Nehemiah. He attacks the evils that arise in Jerusalem after the temple is rebuilt and its services are reestablished. Nehemiah addressed many of these same evils in his written account. Malachi is significant in that his message of judgment on Israel for their continuing sin is the last word from God for 400 years until another prophet arrives with a message from God.

God promises that one day in the future, when the Jews repent, the Messiah will be revealed and God's covenant promises will be fulfilled. The 400 years of silence is broken when John the Baptist preaches, "Repent, for the kingdom of heaven is at hand!" (Matthew 3:2). This was a declaration that the long-promised Messiah (Christ) had come!

The Skeleton

▸ **1:1-5** *The Privilege of God's Love*

Wallowing in the problems of their present condition, the people in

Jerusalem lose their perspective on God's work and His love for them in the past.

▸ **1:6–2:9** *The Pollution of the Priests*

Consumed by greed, the priests were offering only diseased and imperfect animals on the altar and keeping the best for themselves. Because of their disobedience, God withholds His blessings.

▸ **2:10–3:15** *The Problems of the People*

The people are as bad as their priests. They are divorcing their Jewish wives to marry foreign women. They are robbing God of the tithes and offerings due Him, and in arrogance they challenge God's character.

▸ **3:16–4:6** *The Promise of the Lord*

God now spends the rest of the book answering the people's challenge concerning His promises. God says that a day is coming when it will not be "useless to serve God" (3:14), and those who fear God will be blessed. But there is a time coming when the wicked will be judged. The book ends on a bitter note with the word "curse." Although the people had been cured of idolatry, there was little spiritual progress. Sin abounded, and the need for the coming Messiah was greater than ever.

Putting Meat on the Bones

Inspired by Haggai and Zechariah, the Jews have rebuilt the temple. But years have passed and prosperity has not come. They are beginning to question the rewards of being righteous. On the contrary, in a series of questions and answers, God seeks to pierce their stony hearts. In their disobedience, the people question God and want to blame Him for their problems. They thought God's lack of concern was the problem, and said He wasn't following through on His promises.

God answers with stinging rebukes that it is the people's compromise and disobedience that have blocked God's blessings. When they repent and return to God with sincere hearts, the obstacles to divine blessing will be removed.

Life Lessons from Malachi

- God will not bless a disobedient life.
- You cannot out-give God.
- God is true to His promises.
- Apathy results in faithless ritual.

Where to Find It

Reminder of God's love . . . . Chapter 1
Rebuke of the sinful priests . . . . Chapter 2
Robbery of God is cursed . . . . Chapter 3
Return of Christ is prophesied . . . . Chapter 4

Important Prophecies in Malachi

The coming of God's messenger before the Messiah	Malachi 3:1
The second coming of Christ	Malachi 4:2
The prediction that Elijah would announce the Messiah's arrival	Malachi 4:5

The 400 Silent Years

Over 400 years separate the end of the Old Testament from the beginning of the New Testament. Because there is no word from God during these years, they are called the "silent years." However, the history that is predicted in the prophetic book of Daniel continues to move forward with divine precision.

During the span of the 400 silent years the control of the land passes from the Medo-Persian Empire to the Greeks and then to the Romans. The Greeks bring a new trade language to the world, and the Romans bring a system of roads and law and order. Now, at last, the time is right for the coming of Messiah. His message of salvation will be written with precise exactness in the Greek trade language that is in use by most of the known world, and His good news will be communicated and spread throughout the world on the roads built by the Romans.

Even though the voice of God is silent for 400 years, the hand of God is clearly directing the course of history toward the coming of His Son, the Lord Jesus Christ.

The New Testament

The Historical Books

Like the Old Testament, the New Testament is not one book, but a collection of 27 individual books that reflect a wide range of themes, literary forms, and purposes. The first five books in the New Testament—Matthew, Mark, Luke, John (called the Gospels), and Acts—are entirely narrative and the only historical books in the New Testament. The first four books, or the Gospels, are a historical account of the life and times of Jesus Christ, the Messiah, whose birth, life, death, and resurrection were prophesied throughout the Old Testament. The book of Acts provides a factual report of the period from Christ's final words to His followers and His ascension into heaven to the travels and trials of the apostle Paul. Acts describes some of the key events in the spread of the "good news" from Judea to the far reaches of the Roman Empire.

Matthew

Jesus began to preach and to say,
"Repent, for the kingdom of heaven is at hand."
(4:17)

Theme: The kingdom of God
Date: A.D. 60
Author: Matthew (Levi)
Setting: Palestine

It has been 400 years since Malachi gave his last words of prophecy. The world scene has changed. Control of the land of Israel has passed from Medo-Persia to Greece and now to Rome. Greek is still the official trade language of the people, and it is the language in which the New Testament is written. Matthew, whose Jewish name is Levi, is a tax collector until Jesus calls him to become one of the 12 disciples. Now, more than 20 years since Jesus' return to heaven (in Acts 1:9), the good news of Jesus has traveled the length and breadth of the Roman world. The Jewish Christians are starting to be persecuted, and Matthew wants to strengthen their faith and provide them with a useful tool for evangelizing to the Jewish communities dispersed throughout the Roman world. He presents Jesus of Nazareth as Israel's promised Messiah and rightful King. With the King comes His kingdom—the kingdom of heaven—which will be occupied by those who acknowledge and obey this King.

The Skeleton

▸ **Chapters 1–4** *Birth and Preparation of the King*

In these chapters we learn that Jesus, a direct descendant of David, is born of a virgin in fulfillment of prophecy. He is baptized and proclaimed by God as His Son. Jesus' divine character is tested by the devil after 40 days of fasting in the wilderness. Jesus uses Old Testament scripture to counter the devil's temptations. Having passed these tests, He begins His public ministry by preaching repentance and the coming kingdom of God.

▸ **Chapters 5–6** *Sermon on the Mount*

Jesus gathers His disciples on a hillside by the Sea of Galilee and lays out for them in sermon-like fashion the ethics for the kingdom of God. He emphasizes the importance of responding with a heart attitude that goes beyond merely observing a set of rules.

▸ **Chapters 7–20** *Kingdom of God Proclaimed . . . and Rejected*

Through teaching, parables, and performing miracles, Jesus proclaims a new kingdom. He selects 12 disciples (later to become apostles) out of all His followers to share His message. The religious leaders, known as Pharisees and Sadducees, reject Jesus and His message. Jesus foretells His impending death, resurrection, and second coming.

▸ **Chapters 21–25** *Final Clashes with the Religious Leaders*

Jesus enters into the city of Jerusalem with a royal welcome. He confronts the religious leaders, cleanses the temple, and pronounces doom over the city which has rejected God's way. He prophesies the future destruction of the temple, the coming days of tribulation and judgment, and His second coming.

▸ **Chapters 26–28** *Death and Resurrection of Jesus, the King*

After celebrating the Passover feast with His disciples, Jesus is arrested, tried in both religious and secular courts, and crucified. All of this takes place in just several hours. Following His death Jesus is buried, but on the third day, He rises from the dead. He appears to His disciples and commissions them to spread the good news of how He has conquered death.

Putting Meat on the Bones

When Jesus called Matthew, the son of Alphaeus (Mark 2:14), to be one of His disciples, Matthew had a choice to make—Would he give up his prosperous tax-collecting job with the Roman government and follow Jesus...or not? Matthew chose to leave all and become a subject of the King of kings. As a demonstration of this change, Matthew held a big reception for Jesus at his house so that his co-workers could meet Christ and hear about His offer of kingdom citizenship, which Matthew had accepted (Matthew 9:9-13). Later Matthew would write to the whole world about his King—about His miraculous birth, His life and teachings, His miracles, and His triumph over death.

Fleshing It Out in Your Life

Jesus came to earth to die and pay the penalty for our sins, and, with His resurrection, to begin His kingdom reign. His teachings show you how to prepare for life in His kingdom. His kingdom will be fully realized at His return. Until then, all His subjects will be those who faithfully follow Him. The way to enter God's kingdom is by faith—believing in Christ alone to save you from sin. Then God will change you from the inside out to be a citizen of His kingdom. Are you one of His subjects? If so, are you faithfully sharing your King with your co-workers, family, and friends as Matthew did?

Life Lessons from Matthew

- Jesus shows you the Word of God is your best defense against the enemy of your soul.
- Jesus has conquered the power of death and provides the only path to overcoming it.
- Jesus has entrusted His message to His disciples, or His followers. You become a follower when you trust in Him.
- Jesus did not merely preach abstract religious ideas, but a new way of living.
- Jesus is coming again!

Where to Find It

The story of the wise men	Matthew 2:1-12
The temptation of Jesus	Matthew 4:1-11
The Sermon on the Mount	Matthew 5–6
The Beatitudes	Matthew 5:1-12
The parable of the sower and soils	Matthew 13:3-23
The prophecies of the end times	Matthew 24–25
The parable of the talents	Matthew 25:14-30
The great commission	Matthew 28:19-20

The Religious and Political Leaders of Jesus' Day

Scribes—	Jewish experts at the interpretation of Scripture
Rabbis—	Jewish teachers who passed on the scribes' interpretations to the people
Pharisees—	A strict Jewish religious party who understood Scripture as literal, but sought to interpret it using oral traditions
Sadducees—	Wealthy, upper-class descendants of the Jewish high priestly line who rejected the Old Testament except for the five books of Moses
Herodians—	A political party of King Herod's supporters
Zealots—	A fiercely patriotic group of Jews determined to overthrow Roman rule

Mark

The Son of Man
did not come to be served, but to serve,
and to give His life a ransom for many.
(10:45)

Theme: The Suffering Servant
Date written: A.D. 60
Author: John Mark
Setting: Rome

Mark (his Roman name) and John (his Jewish name) was not an eyewitness of the life of Jesus. But he is a close companion of the apostle Peter, who passed on the details of his association with Jesus to John Mark. Whereas Matthew wrote his Gospel to a Jewish audience, Mark seems to target Roman believers. He uses Latin, the language of the Romans, for certain expressions as he writes his Gospel in Greek. Mark describes time according to the Roman system, and carefully explains Jewish customs and omits the traditional Jewish genealogies as found in Matthew. Mark presents Jesus as the Suffering Servant. He focuses more on Jesus' deeds than His teachings. He demonstrates the humanity of Christ and describes His human emotions, His limitations as a human, and ultimately His physical death.

The Skeleton

▸ **Chapters 1–7:23** *Jesus' Ministry in Galilee*

Mark begins immediately with Jesus' ministry years and does not attempt to survey Jesus' life in a detailed, chronological fashion. He instead touches on some key aspects of the Lord's work. Prominent in Mark's account are Jesus' miracles and the rejection He faces from His hometown as well as the Jewish religious leaders.

▸ **Chapters 7:24–10:52** *Jesus Expands His Ministry*

As Jesus visits regions outside of Israel such as Tyre and Sidon, Decapolis, and Bethsaida, He continues to heal people, confirming His credentials as the Messiah promised by the Old Testament prophets. Jesus also predicts His death and warns about the cost of following Him. He then begins to work His way toward Jerusalem, where He will be crucified. Along the way, Jesus proclaims that He "did not come to be served, but to serve, and to give His life a ransom for many" (10:45).

▸ **Chapters 11:1–16:20** *Jesus Arrives in Jerusalem*

The day after Jesus enters Jerusalem, He expresses anger at the money changers and vendors who have set up shop in the temple and overturns their tables. The Jewish religious leaders question Jesus' authority and challenge Him with difficult questions, all of which Jesus answers with great ease and wisdom. Jesus is then arrested, tried, and crucified...and early on the first day of the week, He rises again, and appears first to Mary Magdalene, then to other followers.

Putting Meat on the Bones

Many have asked the question, "Why four Gospels? Couldn't the story of Jesus have been given in one book rather than four?" The apostle John goes the other way and ends his Gospel with the observation that if all that Jesus had done and said had been written down, "even the world itself could not contain the books that would be written" (John 21:25). Each of the Gospel writers gives the story of Jesus from his perspective and for his particular intended audience. As a result, each Gospel contains distinctive material. Taken together, the four Gospels form a complete testimony about Jesus Christ.

Mark's perspective comes from his association with Peter, the disciple who becomes the chief spokesman for this new religious movement. In Mark, the Lord is presented as an active, compassionate, and obedient Servant who constantly ministers to the physical and spiritual needs of others. At the same time Mark clearly shows the power and authority of this unique Servant, showing Him as no less than the Son of God.

Fleshing It Out in Your Life

Following Jesus' example, you should strive to serve God and others. The religious leaders of Jesus' day wanted to be served and rule over others. Jesus taught the exact opposite attitude. Real greatness is shown by service and sacrifice. Ambition, love of power, and position should not be your desire. Instead, seek to be a lowly servant.

Life Lessons from Mark

- Opposition to your beliefs should not keep you from continuing to carry on the work God has called you to do.
- Follow Christ's call and seek a life of self-denial and personal sacrifice.
- Jesus came to serve, and you should desire to follow His example.

Where to Find It

Peter's mother-in-law healed . . . . Mark 1:31
Jesus walks on water . . . . Mark 6:45-52
Jesus cleanses the temple . . . . Mark 11:15-19
Judas agrees to betray Jesus . . . . Mark 14:1-2,10-11

The 12 Disciples

Brothers Peter and Andrew—fishermen

Brothers James and John—fishermen

Philip—fisherman

Bartholomew—also known as Nathanael

Matthew, also known as Levi—a tax collector

Thomas—also known as the twin

James—the son of Alphaeus

Thaddaeus—also known as Judas, son of James

Simon the zealot—a fierce patriot of Judaism

Judas Iscariot—greedy betrayer of Jesus

Luke

The Son of Man has come to seek
and to save that which was lost.
(19:10)

Theme: The Perfect Man
Date written: A.D. 60–62
Author: Luke, the beloved physician
Where written: Rome

It is evident from the opening lines of this Gospel that it is addressed to a man named Theophilus. Its purpose is to give an accurate historical account of the unique life of Jesus. Luke, a doctor and the only Gentile (non-Jew) author of the New Testament books, is writing to strengthen the faith of Gentiles, especially Greek believers. He also desires to stimulate unbelieving Greeks to consider the claims that Jesus Christ is the Perfect Man—the Son of Man—who came in sacrificial service to seek and save sinful men.

The Skeleton

▸ **Chapters 1–4:13** *Jesus' Preparation for Ministry*

In the early chapters of Luke we see the lives of John the Baptist and Jesus intertwined. The two are cousins born months apart, and God commissions John to proclaim the coming of Jesus to save people from their sins. Luke also shares one very rare glimpse into Jesus' childhood years, during which Jesus' parents find Jesus, at age 12, teaching the Jewish religious leaders at the temple, where God's people worshipped in Jerusalem. At around age 30, Jesus is baptized by John the Baptist.

▸ **Chapters 4:14–9:50** *Jesus' Ministry and Miracles in Galilee*

Jesus begins His ministry in His hometown of Nazareth, which is in the region of Galilee. His two primary activities are teaching and healing. It is during this time that Jesus calls His 12 disciples and performs most of His miracles, including raising a widow's dead son, calming the winds and waves on the Sea of Galilee, and casting demons into a herd of swine.

▸ **Chapters 9:51–19:27** *Jesus' Teaching Ministry*

While Jesus continues to do miracles, Luke now presents a greater emphasis on Jesus' ministry of teaching His disciples. In this section, Jesus teaches through many parables, including the parables of the Good Samaritan and the lost sheep. Along the way He teaches many important lessons that are practical for everyday life—lessons about prayer, finances, and faithfulness.

▸ **Chapters 19:28–23:56** *Jesus' Final Week*

Luke provides a survey of Jesus' passion week—His triumphal entry into Jerusalem, His teachings to the Passover crowds, and His last moments with His disciples. After the Last Supper, Jesus is arrested and given mock trials. Though Pilate, the Roman governor, attempts to release Jesus, the crowds want Him crucified. Afterward, Jesus is buried.

▸ **Chapter 24** *Jesus' Final Act—Resurrection!*

But death does not bring an end to Jesus. There is one further act—resurrection! Visitors to the tomb on the third day after the crucifixion, Sunday morning, find it empty and hear the message from two angels that He is risen. The Lord conquers the grave exactly as He promised, and appears on a number of occasions to His disciples before His ascension to heaven and the Father.

Putting Meat on the Bones

Luke shows a strong interest in people and how their lives intersect with Jesus' ministry. This may have been because Luke was a physician trained to care for the physical needs of people. Luke also gives special recognition to women, writing of Mary, Elizabeth, and Anna and their part in the early life of Jesus. Mary and Martha, two sisters from

Bethany, give us a glimpse of home life in New Testament times. The story of Zacchaeus and his desperate desire to see Jesus demonstrates Jesus' concern for even a despised tax collector. Luke's Gospel shows the universality of the Christian message, describing the Son of Man as the compassionate Savior for all people.

Fleshing It Out in Your Life

Jesus' love and compassion should serve as a powerful example to you as you go about your daily life. For example, you need to be like the Good Samaritan that Jesus described in chapter 10, who stopped to help a person who was suffering. And in the same way that Jesus went out of His way to support Mary and Martha after the death of their brother, Lazarus, you too need to go out of your way to support friends and family in their hour of need. No, you are not Jesus, but when you perform acts of love and show compassion, you point others to the Spirit of Jesus, who lives in you.

Life Lessons from Luke

- Jesus shows compassion for the hurting and the lost, and so should you.
- Jesus speaks about the attitudes and actions that should characterize your daily life—forgiveness, faithfulness, thankfulness, and commitment.
- Jesus shows a deep interest in people and their needs. He is not interested in their status, their race, or their gender. You too should develop the same kind of interest in the needs of others, regardless of who or what they are.

Where to Find It

The angelic announcement of Jesus' birth to the shepherds . . . . Luke 2:8-14

The baptism of Jesus . . . . Luke 3:21-22

The temptation of Jesus . . . . Luke 4:1-13

The feeding of 5000 with bread and fish . . . . Luke 9:12-17
The parable of the Good Samaritan . . . . Luke 10:29-37
The parable of the lost sheep and coin . . . . Luke 15:3-10
The parable of the prodigal son . . . . Luke 15:11-32
The widow's mites . . . . Luke 21:1-4
The three denials of Jesus by Peter . . . . Luke 22:54-62

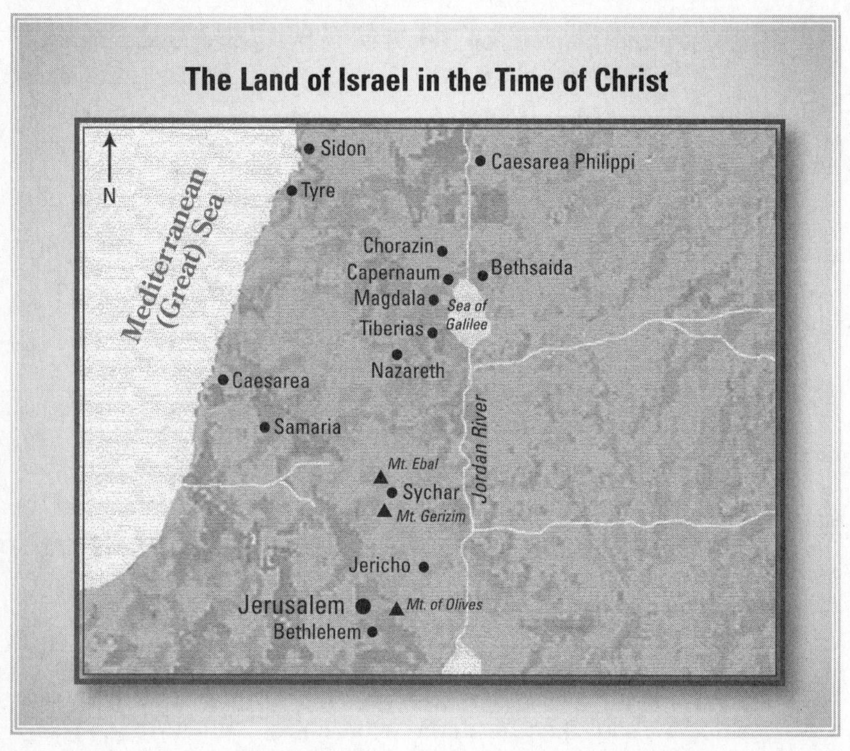

John

These are written that you may believe that
Jesus is the Christ, the Son of God,
and that believing you may have life in His name.
(20:31)

Theme: The Son of God
Date written: A.D. 80–90
Author: John, the disciple whom Jesus loved
Setting: Palestine

It has now been 50 years since John witnessed the earthly life of Jesus. A lot has happened. The Christian faith has flourished and spread throughout the known world. But with growth has come great persecution by the Roman government. All Christ's apostles have died or been martyred except for John. Now an old man, John provides a supplement to what has already been written about Jesus in the first three Gospel accounts. His account of Jesus presents the most powerful and direct case for the deity and humanity of the incarnate Son of God. Taken together with the accounts by Matthew, Mark, and Luke, a reader will have a complete portrait of Jesus, the God-man. In Jesus, perfect humanity and deity are fused, making Him the only possible sacrifice for the sins of mankind.

The Skeleton

▸ **Chapter 1:1-14** *The Incarnation of the Word*

The introduction to John's Gospel reveals that Jesus Christ is the eternal God who became flesh to reveal Himself to His creation and provide spiritual regeneration to those who receive Him.

▸ **Chapters 1:15–11** *The Public Ministry of Jesus*

Jesus performs miracles and dialogues with people such as Nicodemus, the woman at the well, and an adulterous woman about the nature of spiritual reality.

▸ **Chapters 12–17** *The Ministry to Jesus' Disciples*

In the days before His death and resurrection, Jesus focuses on teaching His disciples about His divine assignment, the coming of the Holy Spirit, the importance of being united with Him, and how to live for Him in a hostile world. Jesus then prays a great high-priestly prayer for His followers—that they would see His glory, be protected from the world, and be sanctified and unified so that they may be witnesses who attract others to belief in Christ.

▸ **Chapters 17–21** *The Last Hours and Resurrection of Jesus*

Jesus is arrested, brought to trial, and crucified, all in fulfillment of Scripture. Then, three days later, He rises from the dead. As the Gospel closes, the risen Lord instructs Peter, who had earlier denied Him, to assume responsibility as a leader of this small band of believers and to feed His sheep, or His people.

Putting Meat on the Bones

John gives a precise statement of his purpose in writing: "These are written that you may believe that Jesus is the Christ, the Son of God, and that believing you may have life in His name" (John 20:31). John, with all his heart, wants his readers to "believe" in Jesus as God and Savior. In fact, he uses the term "believe" about 100 times to get the message across. Genesis begins with man made in the image of God, while John begins with God made in the image of man, or as John describes it, "the Word became flesh" (1:14). Jesus is presented as "the Word," the embodiment of the truth, the life, and the glory of the eternal God.

Later John shows the relevance of Jesus' coming to earth in his statement, "God so loved the world that He gave His only begotten Son, that whoever believes in Him should not perish but have everlasting life" (John 3:16). And to further help convince his readers of Jesus' true identity, John organizes his entire Gospel around eight miracles—that is, "signs" or proofs. Only God could perform these miracles. And only the God-man could die as the perfect sacrifice in the place of sinners.

Fleshing It Out in Your Life

Only a fool would ignore road signs on a treacherous mountain road. Likewise, only a spiritual fool would ignore the signs of salvation. Look at the signs that tell you about Jesus Christ—signs that prove He is the Son of God. Do you yet believe? If so, you have life—everlasting life. Don't miss the signs God has placed before you. Pray for eyes that see!

Life Lessons from John

- Jesus is God in flesh, and is the way, the truth, and the life.
- It is only by having a relationship with Jesus that you will experience God.
- You become a child of God by receiving Jesus.
- Jesus can forgive even your most heinous sins.
- Though you fail at times, Jesus extends His forgiveness to you and is willing to take you back.
- Restoration turns uselessness into usefulness.

Where to Find It

The Seven "I Ams" of Jesus

I am the bread of life . . . . John 6:35,48

I am the light of the world . . . . John 8:12; 9:5

I am the door . . . . John 10:7,9

I am the good shepherd . . . . John 10:11,14

I am the resurrection and the life . . . . John 11:25

I am the way, the truth, and the life . . . . John 14:6

I am the true vine . . . . John 15:1,5

Eight Signs of Jesus' Divine Nature

1. Turning water to wine . . . . John 2:1-11
2. Healing the nobleman's son . . . . John 4:46-54
3. Healing the cripple at Bethesda . . . . John 5:1-9
4. Feeding 5000 with five loaves and two fish . . . . . John 6:1-14
5. Walking on water . . . . John 6:15-21
6. Restoring sight to a blind man . . . . John 9:1-41
7. Raising Lazarus from the dead . . . . John 11:1-44
8. Giving the disciples a large catch of fish . . . . . . John 21:1-14

Acts

You shall receive power when the Holy Spirit has come upon you; and you shall be witnesses to Me in Jerusalem, and in all Judea and Samaria, and to the end of the earth.
(1:8)

Theme: The spread of the gospel
Date written: A.D. 60–62
Author: Luke, a Greek physician
Setting: Jerusalem to Rome

Jesus said in Matthew's Gospel that He would build His church, and the gates of hell would not prevail against it. Acts is Luke's account of the growth of the early church. As a sequel to his account of the life of Jesus in the Gospel of Luke, Luke continues the history of what happens after Jesus returned to heaven. He once again addresses his writing to a Greek named Theophilus. In Acts, the church starts with just 120 people in the upper room, where Jesus had the Last Supper with the disciples. But with the coming of the promised Holy Spirit, these few become empowered and boldly witness to all who would listen of the life-changing message of Jesus' resurrection. In spite of severe opposition and persecution, the fearless church experiences explosive growth. Acts 1:8 provides an outline for following Luke's 30-year record of the growth of the church, which begins in Jerusalem, spreads to Samaria, and extends to the world.

The Skeleton

▸ **Chapters 1–7** *The Witness in Jerusalem*

The good news of Jesus' resurrection is to be given first to the Jews. After the Holy Spirit comes upon the followers in the upper room, Peter preaches a powerful sermon and 3000 people respond. Later, after a dramatic healing of a man lame from birth, Peter delivers a second sermon, and thousands more come to believe in Jesus. The religious leaders become threatened by these amazing events and have Stephen—an assistant to the apostles, a server of the widows, and a powerful preacher of the truth—killed as an example to other Christians, hoping to stop their witness and this new religious movement centered on Jesus Christ.

▸ **Chapters 8–12** *The Witness in Samaria*

Stephen's death and the further persecution of Christians did diffuse some of the explosive growth in Jerusalem, but with the scattering of the church, the message about Christ spreads to Samaria, a neighboring region. Peter and John, two of Jesus' disciples, come to the region and confirm that God is at work here. Exercising their authority as apostles of Christ, they impart the Holy Spirit to these new believers.

▸ **Chapters 13–20** *The Witness to the Ends of the Earth*

Luke now switches the focus from Peter to a zealous Pharisee named Paul, who had earlier met the risen Lord Jesus and was converted while on his way to persecute Christians in Damascus. Paul now becomes an eyewitness of the resurrected Christ like the other apostles, and is commissioned by the risen Savior to take the message of His resurrection to the Gentiles. Paul and his team make three missionary journeys on which they plant new churches and train up leaders over a nine-year period.

▸ **Chapters 21–28** *The Witness before Leaders*

As part of his commissioning, Paul was told he was to be Jesus' "chosen vessel...to bear My name before Gentiles, kings, and the children of Israel" (Acts 9:15). In these closing chapters, Paul witnesses before the Jewish council known as the Sanhedrin. He then spends two years in Ceasarea, where he preaches the gospel to two Roman governors and a king before appealing to defend himself before Caesar in Rome. Acts ends with Paul's journey to Rome, where he witnesses to all who will listen while he awaits his trial before Caesar, the ruler of the Roman Empire.

Putting Meat on the Bones

Acts is the historical link between the Gospels and the letters of instruction (the *epistles*) that make up the remainder of the New Testament. Acts is the history of the church and its energizing force, the Holy Spirit. Actually, Acts could be regarded as "the Acts of the Holy Spirit" working in and through the apostles. Luke is not a detached bystander reporting historical facts, but one who is personally involved in the spread of the gospel. Yet he never names himself in his writings. Only occasionally as he writes does Luke include himself in the action with the pronoun *we*.

Fleshing It Out in Your Life

Do you consider yourself part of the "we" when it comes to sharing the gospel? Are you part of the action, or are you a bystander? You have been given the same commission and the same power given to Luke and the early disciples. Don't stand on the sidelines watching others share their faith in the risen Christ. Step out in the power of the Spirit and share what you have seen and heard. Then step back and watch God's Spirit work through your testimony.

Life Lessons from Acts

- Jesus has commissioned you to be His witness.
- The Holy Spirit empowers you to carry out that witness.
- All ministries are important in the church, even "serving tables" in your church.
- You are to faithfully witness of the resurrection and leave the results to God.
- As you witness, you will usually receive one of two responses to the gospel—acceptance or rejection!

Where to Find It

Peter's first sermon . . . . Acts 2:14-39
Peter's second sermon . . . . Acts 3:11-26
The deception by Ananias and Sapphira . . . . Acts 5:1-11
The first deacons chosen . . . . Acts 6:1-7
Paul's conversion . . . . Acts 9:1-18
The conversion of the Gentiles . . . . Acts 10:1-47
Paul stoned and left for dead . . . . Acts 14:19-20
The Council at Jerusalem . . . . Acts 15:1-41
Paul's journey to Rome . . . . Acts 27–28:16

Paul's Three Missionary Journeys

The Three Journeys	*Duration*	*Area of Focus*
Acts 13:2–14:28	one year	Cyprus, Galatia
Acts 15:36–18:22	two years	Corinth
Acts 18:23–21:16	four years	Ephesus

The Doctrinal Books

With the end of Acts and the historical books of the New Testament, the Bible moves to 22 letters (called *epistles*). They are letters of doctrine—teaching and instruction in Christian truth and practice.

The first nine epistles (Romans through 2 Thessalonians) are penned by the same human author, the apostle Paul, and contain many of the doctrines or essentials of the Christian faith. They are all addressed to Christian assemblies, or churches.

The four that follow (1 Timothy through Philemon) are also written by Paul, but are addressed to individuals. Their contents center on personal relationships.

The final nine letters of the New Testament (Hebrews through Revelation) are addressed to groups scattered throughout the world. Their messages address the issues of persecution, false teachers, the superiority of Christ, and His soon return. Even though the book of Revelation focuses largely on God's prophetic plan for the future, it is also a letter of Jesus Christ, transmitted through the apostle John, affirming Christ's authority and His concern for the church. Revelation closes with a wonderful glimpse of the church's future home in heaven.

Romans

In [the gospel of Christ] the righteousness of God is revealed from faith to faith; as it is written, "The just shall live by faith."
(1:17)

Theme: The righteousness of God
Date written: A.D. 56–57
Author: Paul
Setting: Corinth

Toward the close of his third missionary journey, Paul writes this letter to the church in Rome from the Greek city of Corinth. He has come from Ephesus, a city in what is now modern Turkey, where he spent three years planting and strengthening a church. As he prepares to travel to the Jerusalem church with an offering for the poor believers, he stops long enough to write a letter to a church he has never visited. He writes not to correct any doctrinal error, but to introduce himself to the church at Rome so the people can pray for him, encourage him, and help him with his future plans to minister in Spain. But being the teacher he is, Paul can't help but also teach his new friends about the righteousness that comes from God—the great truths of the gospel of grace.

The Skeleton

▸ **Chapters 1–3:20** *The Problem of Righteousness*

Every person in the world is guilty of sin, which separates them from God and condemns all to eternity apart from Him. Even those who are morally good are, at heart, sinners, for "there is none righteous…there is none who seeks after God" (Romans 3:10-11). Therefore, all deserve judgment and condemnation.

▸ **Chapters 3:21–5:21** *The Provision of Righteousness*

God provides the solution to man's problem of sin and judgment by sending Jesus Christ to earth to take the judgment sinners deserve. Jesus, who is perfectly righteous and has no sin, became sin on the cross. He took man's sin and punishment upon Himself, thus freeing those who trust in Him of sin and making them righteous before God.

▸ **Chapters 6–8** *The Power in Righteousness*

Christians—those who believe in Christ as Savior—are declared righteous and possess new life. However, there is still the daily struggle with the sin that resides in the flesh. With the Holy Spirit's help, believers have the power to make right choices and refrain from sin. What's more, for believers, there is no eternal condemnation, and there is nothing that can separate God's children from God's love.

▸ **Chapters 9–11** *The Promise of Righteousness*

Though the people of Israel rejected the Lord Jesus Christ, God's promise to one day redeem and restore Israel still stands. God is not finished with Israel; there is coming a time when Israel's blindness will end, the people will be delivered, and they too will receive the righteousness of God.

▸ **Chapters 12–16** *The Pattern of Righteousness*

Christians have been declared righteous by God. They possess new life through the indwelling of the Holy Spirit. This inner transformation results in an outer transformation. What is true inside a person's heart will show up in a person's life. Some of the signs of a transformed life are yielding to God, submitting to government authority, loving one's neighbor, following Christ's example, bearing others' burdens, and serving diligently.

Putting Meat on the Bones

Paul had often wanted to visit the church in Rome but had been hindered. He had planted many other churches and raised up many new leaders for those churches, and now it is time for him to move on. He wants to travel to and preach in a new area, Spain, and the church at Rome is on the way to Spain. It seems to have been started with believers scattered from Jerusalem after the death of Stephen and the resulting persecution (see Acts 8:1). Paul feels a common bond with the believers in Rome and longs to see them face to face and to pass on to them what he has learned about God's salvation through Jesus Christ. Like an experienced trial lawyer, Paul presents the facts of the gospel and declares that all are lost without God's intervention. Paul then explains that God did intervene by sending His Son, the Lord Jesus Christ, to be the Savior of all who believe. The letter to the Romans is the most forceful, logical, and articulate treatise on salvation ever penned. It goes without saying that the book of Romans has influenced the history of Christianity more than any other epistle.

Who should be given the responsibility of carrying this most important document to Rome? Which one of the leaders should be responsible? How many men should go—two, four, or more? You might be surprised to learn that the task was given to a woman named Phoebe. She is asked by Paul to carry this greatest of all documents hundreds of miles to Rome. What are her qualifications? Only that she is a servant of the church and a faithful helper of many, including Paul.

Fleshing It Out in Your Life

All men and women are sinners. (That includes you and me.) Sin separates mankind from God. But God has graciously extended an offer of salvation to all who place their faith and trust in Christ. Have you accepted God's offer of salvation? If you have, then you possess the righteousness of God in Christ. God now expects you to live a righteous life that honors Him.

Life Lessons from Romans

- Everything you receive as a Christian—your salvation, your justification, your sanctification, and someday your glorification—is a work of God's grace.
- Inward change will produce a corresponding outward fruit. Whatever is true about your heart will show up in your actions.
- The righteousness of God is a gift that can be received only by faith, not earned by your works.
- Faithfulness in the little things will prepare you for greater tasks from God.

Where to Find It

All are without excuse and are accountable to God . . . . Romans 1:18-23
All have sinned . . . . Romans 3:23
Those justified by faith have peace with God . . . . Romans 5:1
The wages of sin is death . . . . Romans: 6:23
There is no condemnation to those in Christ . . . . Romans 8:1
The Holy Spirit prays for believers . . . . Romans 8:26
God has a plan for Israel . . . . Romans 9–11
Present yourself to God as a living sacrifice . . . . Romans 12:1
All are to submit to governing authorities . . . . Romans 13:1-7

The Holy Spirt

His Personhood

- The use of "He" and "Him" (John 14:17)
- His intellect (1 Corinthians 2:11)
- His will (1 Corinthians 12:11)
- His emotions (Ephesians 4:30)
- His fire quenched (1 Thessalonians 5:19)

His Ministry

- His caring for believers (John 14:16,26)
- His convicting of sin (John 16:8-11)
- His guiding (John 16:13)
- His glorifying Christ (John 16:14)
- His choosing (Acts 13:2)
- His directing (Acts 16:6-7)
- His interceding (Romans 8:26-27)
- His sealing of believers (Ephesians 4:30)

1 Corinthians

Whether you eat or drink,
or whatever you do,
do all to the glory of God.
(10:31)

Theme: Christian conduct
Date written: A.D. 55
Author: Paul
Setting: Ephesus

While the apostle Paul is teaching and preaching in Ephesus (a city in what is now modern Turkey) during his third missionary journey, visitors arrive from the church at Corinth, a church he had planted in Greece some three years before. One group of the visitors reports disturbing news of factions, immorality, and lawsuits within the body of believers. Another group comes with difficult questions concerning marriage and divorce, eating food offered to idols, matters of public worship, and the resurrection of the body. Using his God-given power and authority as an apostle—one sent by God as a spokesman—Paul writes this first of two letters to believers in Corinth to firmly address their deplorable conduct and answer their questions.

The Skeleton

▸ **Chapters 1–2** *The Need for True Unity*

Paul is concerned about the divisions and enmity within the Corinthian church. He reminds the people that the message of the cross, empowered by the Holy Spirit, is the basis for true unity.

▸ **Chapter 3** *The Nature of True Spirituality*

Paul points out that as spiritual people, we should not live in a worldly manner. God wants all Christians to remember to whom they belong. That should affect the way they live their lives, for all believers will be judged for their works and rewarded accordingly for their service.

▸ **Chapters 4–11** *The Problems in the Church*

Because many of the believers in the church at Corinth are not living truly spiritual lives, the church has many problems. Paul takes the people to task for devotion to any individual leader (including himself). He condemns them for turning a blind eye to sexual immorality, for bringing legal actions against each other, for neglecting God's teachings on marriage, and for taking the Lord's Supper too lightly.

▸ **Chapters 12–16** *The Resources for Problems*

Then Paul presents teachings intended to help this church get back on track. First he reminds the people that they are all interconnected members of the body of Christ. As such, they all have a variety of gifts to offer each other. These gifts should be exercised in an orderly manner, with love as their prime motivation. Next Paul emphasizes the importance of Christ's resurrection, which is the basis of the people's own coming resurrection. When Christ rose from the dead He defeated death and made possible their salvation. It is the power by which they can live the Christian life.

Putting Meat on the Bones

Paul's letter to the Corinthians is filled with many exhortations for the Corinthian believers to act like Christians. Their most serious problem is worldliness. They are unwilling to let go of the culture around them. They could not consistently separate themselves from their former pagan ways. Their old beliefs were undermining their present behavior.

The corrupt Corinthian culture of Paul's day is much like our culture today. And sadly, the people in many of today's churches display the same spiritual immaturity Paul saw in the Corinthian believers. Immorality, divorce, lawsuits, division, misuse of spiritual gifts, and a lack of love are as much of a problem today as they were then.

Fleshing It Out in Your Life

What's the answer? It's the same for us today as then. Just as Paul attempts to correct the Corinthians through proper teaching, you and I need to correct our behavior with a proper understanding of God's Word. Whether you realize it or not, your behavior is being influenced by your culture, which is filled with wrong kinds of thinking. And wrong living is directly related to wrong thinking. With God's help, bring your behavior back in line with God's standards by reading, studying, and obeying God's Word.

Life Lessons from 1 Corinthians

- God has given you unique "spiritual gifts" to use for the support and growth of the body of Christ.
- Exercising a spiritual gift without showing true love is meaningless.
- God takes sexual immorality very seriously.
- The Lord's Supper is an important celebration and should not be taken lightly.
- Because of the calling God has placed upon their lives, Christian leaders should be treated with respect and honor.
- Christians should not bring lawsuits against each other.

Where to Find It

Discipline for sinning Christians .... 1 Corinthians 5:9-13
Lawsuits in the church .... 1 Corinthians 6:1-7
Sex in marriage .... 1 Corinthians 7:3-5
Divorce .... 1 Corinthians 7:10-16
Marriage and celibacy .... 1 Corinthians 7:25-40
The Lord's Supper .... 1 Corinthians 11:17-34
Instruction on spiritual gifts .... 1 Corinthians 12:4-31

What Is Love?

1 Corinthians 13:4-8

Love is patient.
Love is kind.
Love does not envy.
Love does not parade itself.
Love is not puffed up.
Love does not behave rudely.
Love does not seek its own.
Love is not provoked.
Love thinks no evil.
Love does not rejoice in iniquity.
Love rejoices in the truth.
Love bears all things.
Love believes all things.
Love hopes all things.
Love endures all things.
Love never fails.

2 Corinthians

We do not preach ourselves,
but Christ Jesus the Lord,
and ourselves your bondservants
for Jesus' sake.
(4:5)

Theme: Paul's defense of his apostleship
Date: A.D. 56
Author: Paul
Setting: Philippi (on the way to Corinth)

After writing 1 Corinthians, Paul plans to stay at Ephesus a little while longer before going on to Corinth. His stay, however, is cut short by a riot of the tradesmen over the effect Christianity is having on the sale of idols. Paul sends his young disciples, Titus and Timothy, ahead to find out what effect his exhortations are having on the Corinthian believers. As Paul travels toward Corinth, Titus finds him and reports that the Corinthians have repented of their resistance against Paul and his teaching. With great joy, but filled with concerns regarding new threats and smoldering rebellious attitudes, Paul writes this second letter.

The Skeleton

▸ **Chapters 1–2** *The Personal Testimony of Paul*

Paul's follow-up letter to the Corinthians is a defense of his life and ministry, which some had called into question. He gives thanks to God for bringing him through tough times and giving him great joy. He also reflects on the amazing opportunity Christians have to be Christ's representatives to the world.

▸ **Chapters 3–7** *The Nature of Christian Ministry*

Paul enters into an extended defense of his ministry, pointing to the fruit of his many converts as the credentials for his ministry and the evidence of God's call on his life. He glories in the life-giving power of the gospel to transform hearts and bring true spiritual freedom. Paul encourages believers that, although they will at times suffer for the cause of the gospel, they can be fearless in the face of death because it is not the end. He shares that the nature of true ministry is that it is motivated by Christ's love, is blameless in its actions, and is pure in its lifestyle.

▸ **Chapters 8–13** *The Glory of Christian Ministry*

Hearing from Titus of the Corinthians' repentant hearts, Paul now launches into the longest discussion in the New Testament of the principles and practice of the giving of offerings to support other ministries. Paul also uses his God-given authority, his knowledge, his sufferings, his visions, and his miracles as credentials, urging the rebellious minority in Corinth to repent so he will not have to use severity when he arrives in person.

Putting Meat on the Bones

Titus is overjoyed to inform Paul of the repentant attitude of the Corinthian church, but he also informs Paul that false teachers have arrived with letters of introduction from the church at Jerusalem. With great authority these teachers denounce the position and apostleship of Paul and start preaching false doctrine. Paul acts quickly and sends a second letter to the Corinthians. In it he warns the church against heresies and vindicates his own true apostleship. For this reason, this letter contains more of Paul's personal history than any of his other letters. It is filled with mention of Paul's sufferings and sorrows. He even discusses his "thorn in the flesh" (12:7-10), explaining how God used this trial to keep him humble and teach him God's sufficiency. Through all the suffering, Paul affirms God's faithfulness to provide comfort through His all-sufficient grace. God comforted Paul so that Paul could now comfort others.

Fleshing It Out in Your Life

As you seek to live for Christ, you too will probably be maligned, misunderstood, undermined, and falsely accused. When that happens, do as Paul did. Look to Christ. Recall who you are in Him. Share what God has done in and through you. Rather than dread the trials that are coming your way, take courage in the fact that God is faithful. His strength is sufficient for any trial you are facing or will face in the future. He is the "God of all comfort" (2 Corinthians 1:3), and He promises to comfort you in all your tribulations. But comfort from God is not an end in itself. God comforts you so you can then turn around and comfort others.

Life Lessons from 2 Corinthians

- God has established ministry leaders to shepherd His flock, or His people. These leaders are to be blameless, pure, and dedicated to service, and such leaders are deserving of your honor and respect.
- No Christian—including you—is immune from suffering. In many instances, God's workers suffer more than non-Christians.
- Trials are used by God to teach you humility and dependence on His grace rather than your own strength.
- You should give financially to God's work—sacrificially, with great joy, and with a sense of responsibility.

Where to Find It

God's comfort . . . . 2 Corinthians 1:3-7
Christian giving . . . . .2 Corinthians 8–9
Spiritual warfare . . . . 2 Corinthians 10:3-6
Paul's vision of heaven . . . . 2 Corinthians 12:1-6
Paul's thorn in the flesh . . . . 2 Corinthians 12:7-10

Key Content in...

First Corinthians:

Practical help for Christians

Addresses unbecoming conduct

Answers questions on issues

Advises against worldliness

Adds information on the Last Supper

Assures concerning the resurrection

Second Corinthians:

Personal life of Paul

Shares his heart and love

Answers those accusing him

Warns about false teachers

Supplies reasons for giving

Gives personal experience on suffering

Galatians

Stand fast therefore in the liberty
by which Christ has made us free,
and do not be entangled again
with a yoke of bondage.
(5:1)

Theme: Freedom in Christ
Date written: A.D. 49
Author: Paul
Setting: Antioch

Having just returned from Jerusalem to his home church in Antioch, where the issue of faith in Christ alone for salvation has been affirmed, Paul is shocked by some distressing news. He hears that many of the Galatians who had come to belief in Christ during his first missionary journey have fallen prey to the heresy that Gentile believers must submit to all the Mosaic law before they can become Christians. Paul immediately writes this letter to defend justification by faith alone and warn the churches in Galatia of the dreadful consequence of abandoning the pure gospel of Christ alone for salvation.

The Skeleton

▸ **Chapters 1–2** *Concern for the Pure Gospel*

Paul begins by warning the people in the churches in the southern Galatian cities of Antioch, Iconium, Lystra, and Derbe (Acts 13:14–14:23). He cautions them about those who are not teaching a gospel of faith in Christ alone. These teachers are adding the observance of religious ritual to the gospel, saying these good "works" are necessary in order to please God. But this is legalism, which seeks to gain God's approval through performance. Christ, Paul explains, has already done for us everything that is necessary for our salvation.

▸ **Chapters 3–4** *Defense of the Pure Gospel*

Paul points to Abraham, the great Old Testament leader, and in essence says, "Abraham was not saved by observing religious requirements, but by his belief in God." Because of Abraham's belief, God credited Abraham with righteousness. Paul explains that obeying the law cannot save anyone. In fact, it only condemns people of their sinfulness. Christians are made right with God not through the law, but because of God's grace, which grants salvation and freedom in Christ.

▸ **Chapters 5–6** *Freedom in the Pure Gospel*

Paul instructs the Galatian Christians that they are to enjoy their freedom in Christ and not put themselves in bondage by trying to earn God's favor through religious observances or good deeds. True goodness comes not from self-effort, but from submitting oneself to the Holy Spirit so He can create the fruit of righteousness in a life. When it comes to successful Christian living, no one can boast in their accomplishments, but only in the cross of Christ. Christ made it all possible.

Putting Meat on the Bones

Justification by faith apart from the works of the law is the theme of this urgent letter written by Paul to his friends and fellow believers. Paul divided his argument into three sections with three purposes: 1) He defends his apostolic authority, which affirms his gospel message; 2) he refutes the false teaching of justification through the law by using the Mosaic law itself to teach the principles of justification by faith alone; and 3) he shows that liberty from the law does not mean lawlessness, but instead means that, by God's grace, believers are free to obediently love and serve God.

Fleshing It Out in Your Life

Freedom from an addictive habit or from political oppression is a glorious feeling. Even more exhilarating is the spiritual freedom that comes with faith in Jesus Christ alone. If you are a Christian, you are no longer under the regulations and judgments of the law. Christ has set you free from religious works. There is nothing so thrilling as knowing that your past is forgiven and you are free to live a holy life by the power of the Holy Spirit, who indwells you. However, with freedom comes responsibility. You are responsible to serve your Savior and do His will. You are not free to disobey Christ. Therefore, use your freedom to love and to serve, not to do wrong.

Life Lessons from Galatians

- The gifts of salvation and God's love are given to you purely by God's grace.
- There is nothing you can do to gain favor with God.
- You cannot produce good works on your own, but only with the help of the Holy Spirit.
- When you yield yourself to God, He produces the fruit of the Spirit in your life.
- Christ alone makes possible everything you are as a Christian.

Where to Find It

Paul's three years in Damascus . . . . Galatians 1:17-18
Paul's visit with the Jerusalem Council . . . . Galatians 2:1-10
Paul's confrontation of Peter . . . . Galatians 2:11-21
"I have been crucified with Christ" . . . . Galatians 2:20
The purpose of the law . . . . Galatians 3:19-25
"You are all one in Jesus" . . . . Galatians 3:28
The command to walk by the Spirit . . . . Galatians 5:16-18
The fruit of the Spirit . . . . Galatians 5:22-23
The principle of sowing and reaping . . . . Galatians 6:7

The Works of the Flesh

Galatians 5:19-21

Adultery	Fornication
Uncleanness	Lewdness
Idolatry	Sorcery
Hatred	Contentions
Jealousies	Outbursts of wrath
Selfish ambitions	Dissensions
Heresies	Envy
Murders	Drunkenness
Rivalries	And the like

The Fruit of the Spirit

Galatians 5:22-23

Love	Joy
Peace	Longsuffering
Kindness	Goodness
Faithfulness	Gentleness
Self-control	

Ephesians

Blessed be the God and Father
of our Lord Jesus Christ,
who has blessed us with every spiritual blessing
in the heavenly places in Christ.
(1:3)

Theme: Blessings in Christ
Date written: A.D. 60–62
Author: Paul
Setting: A Roman prison

One of the most prominent early churches was the church in Ephesus. Paul founded the church and spent three years teaching its members. Now, some five or six years later, Paul is a prisoner in Rome, awaiting a trial before Caesar. While he waits, Paul writes this letter. Unlike some of his other letters, this one is not written to speak of some heresy or specific problem in the church. Instead, Ephesians is a letter of encouragement. In it Paul describes the nature of the church, which is not an *organization* but a living *organism*, the body of Christ. He then challenges his readers to function as the living body of Christ on earth.

The Skeleton

▸ **Chapters 1–3** *The Powerful Blessings in Christ*

Paul opens his epistle with a remarkable list of the spiritual blessings that have been given to every believer. Believers in Christ are chosen by God, redeemed by Christ, and given a heavenly inheritance through Christ. They have been adopted, redeemed, and given grace and citizenship. Through the power of the Holy Spirit they can experience the fullness of life in Christ. Each believer is a part of Christ's body, the church. God is building His people into a temple for His dwelling. Paul prays that his readers would receive spiritual understanding so that they would come to perceive what is in fact true of their position in Christ—they possess power!

▸ **Chapters 4:1–5:20** *The Power to Live*

Paul now changes from emphasizing ***doctrine*** in the first three chapters to focusing on ***duty,*** and how it is to be performed, in the last three chapters. Paul explains that through the power of the Spirit, believers are to put off the old self and live by the new self. This worthy walk of love leads to a holiness in lifestyle as Christians become imitators of God. This is what the Spirit-filled life is all about.

▸ **Chapters 5:21–6:9** *The Power to Love and Work*

In the same way that Christ loved His church, husbands are to love their wives, and wives are to willingly submit to the godly leadership of their husbands. Life in Christ also means children are to obey their parents and parents are to lead their children with love and discernment. Finally, slaves (or, in today's society, workers) are to be submissive to their employers, doing their work as if they were working for Christ. Paul doesn't omit masters or bosses, but challenges them to lead properly, knowing that their ultimate master is Jesus Christ.

▸ **Chapter 6:10-24** *The Power for the Battle*

As believers walk with Christ, they will meet resistance from the enemy of their souls—the devil. However, they have weapons that God has provided for use against the devil's temptations and attacks. These weapons are spiritual in nature, and not physical. They are faith, prayer, and the Word of God. With these spiritual weapons, Christians can fight life's battles and be victorious!

Putting Meat on the Bones

Paul writes this epistle to the Ephesian church to make the members more aware of their spiritual resources. He uses the first three chapters to describe where these resources come from—their relationship with Christ and their position in Him. Paul then spends the last three chapters encouraging his readers to draw upon those resources so they can live their Christian lives in a victorious manner. Put another way, the first half of the epistle describes a believer's *wealth* in Christ, and the last half challenges a believer's *walk* in Christ.

Fleshing It Out in Your Life

Everyone who has trusted in Christ possesses an endless supply of *spiritual blessings*. Unfortunately, most believers act as though they are *spiritual beggars* and live in defeat. Why is this so? Many are unaware of all the resources that are theirs in Christ, and therefore fail to appropriate those divine resources. Do you understand what your resources are in Christ? If not, Ephesians will help you find out. If you do know what your resources are, then start or continue to "walk worthy of the calling with which you were called" (Ephesians 4:1).

Life Lessons from Ephesians

- Remember that it is only in Christ that you can grow and mature spiritually.
- God has given you the tools you need to fight against the enemy.
- You must use God's resources to obtain spiritual victory.
- All your work is to be done as to the Lord.
- God has created an order that you are to follow for success in your family life.

Where to Find It

Grieving the Spirit . . . . Ephesians 4:30
Redeeming the time . . . . Ephesians 5:15-16
Roles and responsibilities in marriage . . . . Ephesians 5:22-33
Roles of children and parents . . . . Ephesians 6:1-4
Roles of bosses and workers . . . . Ephesians 6:5-9
Spiritual armor of the believer . . . . Ephesians 6:10-17

The Armor of God

Ephesians 6:14-17

The waistband of truth
The breastplate of righteousness
The shoes as the gospel of peace
The shield of faith
The helmet of salvation
The sword of the Spirit, the word of God

Philippians

Rejoice in the Lord always.
Again I will say, rejoice!
(4:4)

Theme: The joy-filled life
Date written: A.D. 62
Author: Paul
Setting: Prison

It has now been four or five years since Paul made his last visit to Philippi, where he planted a church during his second missionary journey. The Philippian church had always given funds to help finance Paul's needs, and this was no exception. Having heard about Paul's imprisonment, they send another contribution, and along with it, a man named Epaphroditus to minister personally to Paul's needs. Unfortunately, Epaphroditus becomes ill, almost to the point of death. Paul, who realizes his own death could be close, writes this letter to thank the Philippians for their gift. Out of concern for Epaphroditus and fear that the Philippians might be worried about their dear messenger, Paul decides to send Epaphroditus home along with this letter. In the letter Paul describes his circumstance in prison, exhorts the believers in Philippi toward greater unity, and warns them against false teachers.

The Skeleton

▸ **Chapter 1** *Paul's Difficult Circumstances*

Even though Paul is in chains, he is not discouraged because, as he says, his circumstance has "turned out for the furtherance of the gospel"

(Philippians 1:12). Paul is confident that Christ will be glorified even if he dies for his faith in Christ, and affirms that good can come from suffering for Christ's sake.

▸ **Chapter 2:1-18** *Paul's Loving Encouragement*

Paul begins the teaching portion of Philippians by encouraging believers to live in unity with one another. The key to unity is to be likeminded and serve others, rather than selfish and preoccupied with self. Christians are to follow in the steps of Christ, who is the supreme example of humility—He was willing to die on the cross for our benefit.

▸ **Chapter 2:19-30** *Paul's Faithful Friends*

Next Paul expresses his deep appreciation for Timothy, who is of proven character and has served alongside Paul with diligence. Paul hopes to send this likeminded man to the Philippians soon. But Paul does not want to forget to praise Epaphroditus, who ministered to Paul to the point of exhaustion and became sick. These two friends, Timothy and Epaphroditus, are examples of the self-sacrifice that ought to mark our lives as Christians.

▸ **Chapter 3:1–4:1** *Paul's Firm Warnings*

The Christian journey is not an easy one. The Philippians can expect opposition, and they will need to persevere and press toward the goal of spiritual growth and maturity. When life becomes discouraging here on earth, they need to remember that they are citizens of heaven, which is their real home.

▸ **Chapter 4:2-23** *Paul's Final Exhortations*

Though life is difficult, Paul says believers in Christ should not be anxious or allow negative thoughts to pull them down. Rather, they are encouraged to rejoice in the Lord and to give everything to Him in prayer. When they do, the peace of God will guard their hearts.

Putting Meat on the Bones

The key word in this letter is "joy." In one form or another, it is used 19 times. When Paul wrote, "Rejoice in the Lord always" (4:4), he was not sitting in comfort or in pleasant surroundings. Instead, he was a captive in a Roman prison. Yet Paul could rejoice even while in prison because of his passion for knowing Jesus Christ more and more. This is the secret of a joyful Christian life. Joy is not based on circumstances, but in the confidence that comes from a relationship with Jesus Christ.

Fleshing It Out in Your Life

Everyone wants to be happy. Therefore many people make it a lifelong pursuit by spending money, traveling to new places, and experiencing new and exciting activities. But this kind of happiness depends on positive circumstances. What happens when your circumstances are not so positive or joyous? Often your happiness disappears and despair sets in. In bold contrast to happiness stands joy. You have joy because you know that God is at work in your life in spite of your circumstances. True joy comes from knowing Christ personally and from depending on His strength rather than your own. Do you know true joy and contentment? Do you know Christ personally, and are you depending on His strength rather than your own?

Life Lessons from Philippians

- Difficult circumstances should not prevent you from sharing the gospel.
- Christ humbly sacrificed Himself for the good of others, and you are called to follow His example.
- Unity comes when you put others above yourself and care for their needs.
- You are commanded not to worry, but rather to give all your concerns to God and allow Him to take care of them.
- Even your most difficult circumstances can have positive benefits and be a cause for rejoicing.

Where to Find It

God will finish what He begins in you . . . . Philippians 1:6
To live is Christ, and to die is gain . . . . Philippians 1:21
Christ is your example of humility . . . . .Philippians 2:5-11
Everyone will confess Jesus as Lord . . . . .Philippians 2:10-11
You may know Christ and His power . . . . Philippians 3:10
Your citizenship is in heaven . . . . Philippians 3:20
You are to rejoice always . . . . Philippians 4:4
You can do all things through Christ . . . . Philippians 4:13
God will supply all your needs . . . . Philippians 4:19

Christ in Philippians

Christ is our life (1:21)

Christ is our model of humility (2:5)

Christ is our hope (3:21)

Christ is our strength (4:13)

Colossians

In Him dwells all the fullness
of the Godhead bodily;
and you are complete in Him....
(2:9-10)

Theme: The supremacy of Christ
Date written: A.D. 60–61
Author: Paul
Setting: Prison

Colosse was a small city about 100 miles east of Ephesus. The founding pastor of the church in Colosse there was not Paul but a man named Epaphras, who had been converted by Paul while on a visit to Ephesus. Paul had ministered in Ephesus for three years on his third missionary journey. Paul had never visited the church in Colosse, but Epaphras has now come to Rome to visit Paul and report his concerns about a heretical philosophy that is being taught in Colosse. Paul immediately pens this letter to warn the Colossians against this heresy that is devaluing Christ. He writes to give them a proper understanding of Christ's attributes and accomplishments.

The Skeleton

▸ **Chapter 1:1-14** *The Heart of Paul*

Paul greets the Christians in Colosse by thanking God for the spiritual fruit on display in their lives and by praying that they would be filled with the knowledge of God's will for their lives. When believers know and understand God's desires for them, they are able to be spiritually productive.

▸ **Chapters 1:15–2:7** *The Truth about Christ*

Apparently some false teachers in Colosse were saying there was more to the Christian life than Christ—that it was necessary to also gain some kind of "deeper knowledge" and observe certain religious traditions. Paul warns of these serious errors and says that Christ is all one needs. Christ alone is the head of the church, the hope of future glory, and the source of true wisdom and knowledge.

▸ **Chapter 2:8-23** *The Believer's Sufficiency in Christ*

The false teachers in Colosse are encouraging the Christians to seek some kind of higher knowledge and observe certain regulations. Paul argues that believers are already complete in Christ in every way, including their salvation. There is no need for them to bind themselves to legalistic regulations.

▸ **Chapters 3–4** *The Believer's Character in Christ*

Rather than follow man-made rules that give a false sense of religious superiority, Paul instructs that Christians are called to put aside their earthly ways (anger, malice, bad language, lying, and so on) and put on the character of the new man—mercy, kindness, humility, meekness, longsuffering, forbearance, and forgiveness. In their lives, their homes, and their work, believers are to live as God-pleasers, not men-pleasers.

Putting Meat on the Bones

Paul wants the Colossians to understand the implications of the supremacy of Christ. First he explains that a proper view of Christ is the antidote for heresy. Christ is sufficient. Nothing else needs to be added if one has Christ as Savior. Second, since Christ is supreme, the believers in Colosse are to live in obedience to Christ both in behavior and attitude. They are to be merciful, kind, humble, meek, patient, forgiving, and loving.

Fleshing It Out in Your Life

Because Christ is supreme, submission is not optional. As you are obedient to His commands, He provides the basis and power for the transformation of every area of your life, including your home and your job. Is Christ supreme in your life? Read the epistle of Colossians and gain a better appreciation and understanding of the sufficiency of your Savior for your every area of need.

Life Lessons from Colossians

- When it comes to salvation and living the Christian life, the Lord Jesus Christ has done it all for you.
- You are totally sufficient in Christ and have no need of special or unique knowledge, experiences, or religious regulations.
- Christ is supreme, and your commitment to Him should be total.
- Living the Christian life means you put off the qualities of the world and put on the character of Christ.

Where to Find It

Do not lie to one another . . . . Colossians 3:9
Bear with one another . . . . Colossians 3:13
Forgive one another . . . . Colossians 3:13
Admonish one another . . . . Colossians 3:16

Christ in Colossians

Christ is our redemption (1:14)
Christ is the embodiment of deity (1:15)
Christ is the Creator and Sustainer of all things (1:16-17)
Christ is head of the church (1:18)
Christ is the author of reconciliation (1:20)
Christ is the basis of our hope (1:27)
Christ is the source of power for living (1:29)

1 Thessalonians

If we believe that Jesus died and rose again,
even so God will bring with Him
those who sleep in Jesus.
(4:14)

♁

Theme: Concern for the church
Date written: A.D. 51
Author: Paul
Setting: Corinth

It is not clear exactly how long Paul was in Thessalonica, a city in northern Greece. It could have been as little as three weeks. But because of the quick response Paul's message of salvation in Christ received from many God-fearing Gentiles, jealous Jews quickly turned the townspeople against Paul. To avoid the mob, Paul had to flee under the cover of darkness. Still concerned for these new believers, Paul sends his companion Timothy to see how they are doing while he travels on to Athens and Corinth. Timothy meets Paul in Corinth, and the book of 1 Thessalonians is the result of Timothy's good report from this new church.

The Skeleton

▸ **Chapter 1** *Paul's Evaluation of the Church*

The witness of the church in Thessalonica had quickly spread throughout the entire region, so much so that as Paul traveled along, he had no need to say anything about the church. Paul takes great pride in the spiritual health of this new church as seen by their missionary zeal, their dedication to the truth, their conduct in the face of persecution, their unselfish love, and their devotion to ministry.

▸ **Chapters 2–3** *Paul's Conduct and Concern*

Paul reviews how he and his companions, Silas and Timothy, brought the gospel to those in Thessalonica, how they accepted the message, and how he now longs to be with them again. Because of his ongoing concern, he again sends Timothy back to encourage them in their Christian faith. Even though Paul had earlier received positive reports on the state of this church from Timothy, he ends with a prayer for even greater growth in Christ among the Thessalonians.

▸ **Chapter 4:1–12** *Paul's Exhortation*

This chapter begins the central thrust of Paul's message. Paul reminds the Thessalonians to continue to please God in their daily lives by avoiding sexual sin, loving one another, and living as good citizens in a secular world.

▸ **Chapters 4:13–5:28** *Paul's Reminder of the Believer's Hope*

Even though Paul's ministry in Thessalonica was brief, the new church had already come to believe in and hope for the reality of their Savior's return. Paul reminds them of the blessed hope that Jesus is coming again. Therefore, "the day of the LORD" can be a day of rejoicing rather than a day of judgment. Paul closes with an exhortation for the people to honor their church leaders for their labor among them, and for wisdom as to how they are to treat each other. Paul ends with a benediction that God would keep them holy until Christ's return.

Putting Meat on the Bones

The Thessalonian Christians are living in expectation of the soon return of Christ. Paul has taught them that Christ's second coming is the culmination of redemptive history. For that reason, the Thessalonians did not want to miss it! Timothy brings back news that they are concerned because some of the Christians among them have already died. They wonder, *Will these departed souls miss Christ's return?* Paul informs them that the deceased believers haven't missed out on Jesus' return, and assures them that even their dead will participate in Christ's return.

Fleshing It Out in Your Life

No one knows the time of Christ's return. However, one day all believers, both those who are alive and those who have died, will be united with Christ. Daily anticipation of His return should comfort you as you deal with your everyday difficulties. Knowing that Christ will return should motivate you to live a holy and productive life. So live in expectation of Christ's return at any moment. Don't be caught unprepared.

Life Lessons from 1 Thessalonians

- You are to esteem and honor your church leaders.
- Your testimony is a powerful witnessing tool.
- Godly living will evoke persecution.
- The promised return of Christ should motivate you toward holy living.

Where to Find It

A picture of a model church . . . . 1 Thessalonians 1:8-10
A picture of Paul's ministry . . . . 1 Thessalonians 2:1-12
Timothy's report on the church . . . . 1 Thessalonians 3:6-10
The second coming of Christ . . . . 1 Thessalonians 4:13-18
The day of the Lord . . . . 1 Thessalonians 5:1-4
The frequency of prayer .1 Thessalonians 5:17
The quenching of the Spirit .1 Thessalonians 5:19

The Details of Christ's Second Coming

Christ is preparing a place in heaven (John 14:1-3)

Christ's coming will be rapid (1 Corinthians 15:51-52)

Christ will descend from heaven… (1 Thessalonians 4:16)

…with a shout

…with the voice of an archangel

…with the sounding of the trumpet of God

Christ's coming will cause... (1 Thessalonians 4:16-18)

...the dead in Christ to be raised first

...those believers who are alive to be "caught up"

...both those dead and alive to meet the Lord in the air

...all to be with the Lord forever

2 Thessalonians

The Lord is faithful,
who will establish you and guard you
from the evil one.
(3:3)

Theme: Living in hope
Date written: A.D. 52
Author: Paul
Setting: Corinth

This is a sequel to Paul's first letter to the Thessalonian believers. It is written just a few months later while Paul is in Corinth. Word came to Paul from Thessalonica that some have misunderstood his teaching about the second coming of Christ. His statements that Christ could come at any moment had caused some to stop working at their jobs and to begin sitting around waiting for Christ's return. Others are viewing their continuing persecution as signs that this must be "the day of the LORD," or the last days. Responding quickly, Paul sends this second epistle to the young church.

The Skeleton

▸ **Chapter 1** *Paul Comforts the Discouraged*

As he did in the first letter, Paul commends the Thessalonians for their faith in Christ. Then he consoles these victims of suffering and persecution with the knowledge that when Christ returns, He will reward the faithful and punish the wicked. He prays that God will be glorified through their faithful service.

▸ **Chapter 2** *Paul Corrects a Misunderstanding*

Paul clarifies the error made by those who believed that "the day of the LORD" had already come and warns that mass apostasy and rebellion will occur before that day. That day, Paul writes, will be characterized by the rise of "the man of sin" and others who practice deception and reject the truth. Meanwhile Paul offers up a prayer that the Thessalonian believers will stand firm in their faith.

▸ **Chapter 3** *Paul Condemns Idleness*

Paul begins this last section of his letter with a request for prayer that the gospel would spread swiftly and that God, who is faithful, will continue to guard them from the evil one.

Paul then finishes with a word of warning for those believers who have stopped working and have built their life around waiting for the Lord's second coming. Paul is very clear that the anticipation of Jesus' return should not keep believers from fulfilling the basic responsibilities of life, including work. He uses himself as an example of one who worked for his food while he was with the Thessalonians instead of relying on others to meet his practical, daily needs.

Putting Meat on the Bones

Even when people try their best to be clear in their communications, misunderstandings can occur, especially if a person is prone to interpret words through personal biases or prejudices. That's what happened with Paul's first letter to the Thessalonians. Some people had become discouraged because they thought their present persecution meant they had missed the Lord's return, that they were actually in "the day of the LORD" and experiencing the awful tribulation promised in that day. They did not understand that persecution is always to be expected by those who are aggressive about their faith in the Lord. And for others, the expectation of the imminent return of Christ had given them an excuse for laziness.

Fleshing It Out in Your Life

Paul's letter should help you not to become discouraged or afraid when you are persecuted or see evil on the increase. God is still in control, no matter how desperate things look or become. He has a plan for your future, and this hope should give you strength and assurance to keep moving forward instead of stopping and doing nothing. Paul's encouragement is that you stand firm, keep working, keep doing good, and keep waiting for Christ.

Life Lessons from 2 Thessalonians

- Your anticipation of Christ's return should not keep you from living life in a responsible manner.
- God is with you in your suffering and will use it to bring glory to Himself.
- Make sure you properly understand what Scripture says, for it will affect how you live.
- God expects you to provide for yourself and your family's physical needs, and not expect others to make up for your lack of responsibility.

Where to Find It

Comfort in persecution .... 2 Thessalonians 1:5-12
Second coming of Christ .... 2 Thessalonians 2:1-12
Profile of a Christian .... 2 Thessalonians 2:13-17
Paul's request for prayer ....2 Thessalonians 3:1
Warning against laziness .... 2 Thessalonians 3:6-15

Profile of "the Man of Sin"

• Called "the son of perdition"	2 Thessalonians 2:3
• Called the "little" horn	Daniel 7:8
• Called "the prince who is to come"	Daniel 9:26
• Called "the Antichrist"	1 John 2:18
• Called "the beast"	Revelation 13:2-10

Details from 2 Thessalonians 2:3-12 About "the Man of Sin"

- He comes with a great apostasy.
- He is held in check until "the restrainer"—the Holy Spirit—is taken out of the way.
- He proclaims himself to be God.
- He sits in the temple of God.
- His coming is the work of Satan.
- His coming is with power, signs, lying wonders, and deception.
- He will be consumed by the breath of God.

1 Timothy

If I am delayed, I write so that you may know how you ought to conduct yourself in the house of God, which is the church of the living God.
(3:15)

Theme: Instructions for a young disciple
Date written: A.D. 64
Author: Paul
Setting: Macedonia/Philippi

Timothy has been one of Paul's closest disciples since he was first recruited by Paul for service some 15 years earlier. Paul has just been released from his first imprisonment in Rome, and revisits several of the cities in which he had ministered, including Ephesus. When Paul leaves Ephesus, he asks Timothy to stay behind as his personal representative. Paul then goes on to Macedonia, while Timothy now finds himself serving as pastor of the church at Ephesus. Paul hopes to eventually return to Timothy, but in the meantime, he writes this letter to give Timothy practical advice for his pastoral ministry.

The Skeleton

▸ **Chapter 1** *Instruction about False Doctrine*

Paul immediately opens with a warning about the growing problem of false doctrine, particularly in relation to Jewish interpretations of the Old Testament and the misuse of the law of Moses. Paul writes that the law is good because it reflects God's holy and righteous standard. Its purpose is to show people their sin and their need for the saving gospel of

Jesus Christ. At this point the aging apostle and servant of God rehearses his dramatic conversion and his calling to the ministry. He also reminds Timothy of his own divine calling and charges Timothy to fulfill it without wavering in doctrine or conduct.

▸ **Chapters 2–3** *Instruction about the Church*

Having given Timothy his marching orders, Paul now addresses some issues about church worship. Public prayer should be a part of the worship service and should be the role of the men in the church. The women, on the other hand, should not teach or have authority over the men in the worship service, but rather, focus on developing the inner quality of godliness. Next Paul addresses the qualifications of two groups of leaders—bishops (or overseers) and deacons.

▸ **Chapter 4** *Instruction about False Teachers*

Having already warned of false teachers, Paul now describes the characteristics of false teachers, how to recognize them, and how to respond to them. Paul also explains that God's teachers, by contrast, defend their flock by consistently proclaiming God's truth. This is what Paul exhorts Timothy to do as well.

▸ **Chapter 5** *Instruction about the Pastorate*

Next, Paul gives practical advice on the pastoral care of the young, the old, and the widows. He also addresses the proper honor due to church leaders (called "elders" here but "bishops" earlier) and the process of selecting them.

▸ **Chapter 6** *Instruction about Worldliness*

Paul concludes by describing the motives of false teachers. They are in ministry for personal profit; they are greedy. By contrast, Timothy is told to guard his motives when it comes to money, to stand firm in his faith, to live above reproach, and to exhort the rich to share their wealth.

Putting Meat on the Bones

Bank tellers are taught to spot counterfeit bills by becoming very familiar with the genuine article. This same technique applies to detecting false teachers and their wrong teachings. We must know the truth in order to spot error. Timothy knew the truth, for he had heard Paul preach and teach for 15 years. Therefore it was only natural for Paul to give Timothy the responsibility of defending the faith by teaching the truth. Armed with sound doctrine, the Ephesians could defend themselves against counterfeit teachers and their false teachings.

Fleshing It Out in Your Life

Do you know the truths in God's Word well enough to spot a false teacher or false teaching? Are you prepared to defend the Christian faith with your present level of biblical knowledge? If so, follow Paul's example and find younger-in-the-faith Christians and begin mentoring them. If you are not as mature as you would like to be, follow the example of Timothy and gain wisdom by learning from a more mature Christian.

So much is at stake! False teaching is much more harmful than a counterfeit dollar bill. A false dollar only affects you physically. But false teaching affects the soul. Paul calls false doctrine the "doctrines of demons" (1 Timothy 4:1). Get to know your Bible both on your own and with the help of a mentor so you can defend your faith and protect your family and others from the worst of all errors—spiritual error.

Life Lessons from 1 Timothy

- If you are a church leader or one who aspires to that position, measure yourself against the spiritual qualifications of elders and deacons.
- If you are a discipler or mentor, take note of the relationship Paul had with his young disciple. Paul gave guidance and counsel not for just a few weeks or months, but for years!
- If you are young in the faith, follow the example of Timothy, who imitated the life of his mentor, Paul.
- If you are a parent, remind yourself of the profound effect a strong Christian home can have on your children.

Where to Find It

The roles of men and women in public worship . . . . 1 Timothy 2:8-15
The qualifications for a bishop/elder . . . . 1 Timothy 3:1-7
The qualifications for a deacon . . . . 1 Timothy 3:8-13
The profile of an apostate . . . . 1 Timothy 4:1-3
The financial support of widows . . . . 1 Timothy 5:9-16
The financial support of elders . . . . 1 Timothy 5:17-21
The sinful love of money . . . . 1 Timothy 6:6-10

The Titles and Qualifications of Leaders in the New Testament

Bishop or overseer	1 Timothy 3:1-7
Elder	Titus 1:5-9
Pastor	1 Peter 5:2

(Note: The above terms for leaders are used for those in the church who feed, lead, watch over, and warn God's people—see Acts 20:28-32. These terms are also used interchangably in the New Testament.)

Deacon or server	Acts 6:1-6; 1 Timothy 3:8-13

2 Timothy

Be diligent to present yourself approved to God,
a worker who does not need to be ashamed,
rightly dividing the word of truth.
(2:15)

Theme: A charge to faithful ministry
Date written: A.D. 67
Author: Paul
Setting: Rome

Paul is in prison and alone except for the presence of Luke, who has been his faithful friend and personal physician for many years. Paul is also aware that the end is near. But before he dies, Paul wants to pass on the mantle of ministry to Timothy, his trusted assistant. Concerned that Timothy may be in danger of spiritual burnout, Paul writes to encourage him to continue being faithful to his duties, to hold on to sound doctrine, to avoid error, to expect persecution for preaching the gospel, and above all, to put his confidence in the Word of God as he preaches it constantly.

The Skeleton

▸ **Chapter 1** *The Prerequisites for Faithful Ministry*

Paul opens his letter to his "beloved son" (1:2) with tenderness and love. He reminds Timothy of his assets for the ministry—a genuine faith that had been modeled for him by his mother and grandmother, his calling and giftedness, a resolve to hold tightly to the truth of God's Word, and a loyalty that will last even under the most difficult of circumstances.

▸ **Chapter 2** *The Pattern for Faithful Ministers*

After affirming Timothy's assets for ministry, Paul now challenges Timothy to prepare others to follow him in the ministry. Timothy is to discipline himself like a soldier, an athlete, and a farmer, and to follow Paul's example of endurance. In his dealings with others, Timothy must not get entangled in useless controversies. In his dealings with himself, he must flee youthful lust and keep his life pure.

▸ **Chapter 3** *The Perils of Faithful Ministry*

Paul, the ever-vigilant leader, anticipates perilous times of growing apostasy and wickedness, during which men and women will be increasingly susceptible to false teaching. And Paul exhorts Timothy to never waver in his use of the Scriptures to combat this growing problem. In fact, it was these same Scriptures that God had used even in Timothy's childhood to made Timothy "wise for salvation" (2 Timothy 3:15). These Scriptures are "God-breathed" and will now equip Timothy to combat erroneous teaching and heresy.

▸ **Chapter 4** *The Proclamation of Faithful Ministers*

Paul's final exhortation to Timothy is that a man of God must be ready to preach the Word of God at any time and at any place in all the ways necessary to reach deceived people. Paul closes this very personal letter with an update on his situation in Rome. He states his longing to see Timothy before the end, and asks him to come to Rome and bring certain articles, particularly what he calls "the parchments" (1 Timothy 4:13), probably portions of the Old Testament.

Putting Meat on the Bones

If you knew you were going to die in the near future, what information would you want to pass on, and who would you want to pass it on to? That was Paul's situation. He was on "death row," waiting his execution for preaching the gospel of Christ. The letter of 2 Timothy is his last will and testament. Of all the people Paul has known over the years, he chooses to write one last letter to his spiritual son in the faith, Timothy. Instead of trying to drum up sympathy or pity for himself or stir up reprisals against an unjust and godless governmental system, Paul writes to comfort and encourage and motivate Timothy.

Paul's message to Timothy has also come to the rescue of other distressed Christian workers down through the centuries. He reminds all Christian workers of what is truly important and what will ultimately provide strength and power—the Word of God. To the very end, Paul is thinking of the personal and spiritual needs of others more than he is thinking of himself.

Fleshing It Out in Your Life

How does Paul's utter disregard for himself strike you? Are you so busy focusing on yourself and your perceived needs that you are failing to notice the truly needy people around you? Look outside yourself. You are sure to find plenty of desperate people who could use a helping hand or a word of encouragement, particularly a message from God's Word delivered to them...by you!

Life Lessons from 2 Timothy

- Your Christian life is to be a disciplined life.
- Your sincere faith can have a profoundly positive effect on your family and others.
- As a corollary, hypocritical faith can have an equally profound and negative effect.
- Scripture, empowered by God's Spirit, is the instrument that brings people to salvation.
- Scripture is essential for encouraging a life of godliness.
- Mentoring, as modeled by Paul, is a lifelong commitment.

Where to Find It

"God has not given us a spirit of fear" . . . . .2 Timothy 1:7
"I know whom I have believed" . . . . .2 Timothy 1:12
The mandate for discipleship . . . . .2 Timothy 2:2

A diligent workman for God is not ashamed . . . . .2 Timothy 2:15
The inspiration of Scripture . . . . 2 Timothy 3:16-17
"I have fought the good fight" . . . . 2 Timothy 4:6-8

The Word of God Is Important

2 Timothy 3:16-17

Because It Is...

- Inspired by God—it is God-breathed
- Profitable for doctrine—it instructs in divine truth
- Essential for reproof—it rebukes wrong behavior
- Necessary for correction—it points the way back to godly living
- Helpful for instruction in righteousness—it trains in right behavior
- Able to make you complete—it is capable of making you proficient in all you do
- Always there to equip you—it prepares you for the demands of righteous living

Titus

As for you, speak the things
which are proper for sound doctrine.
(2:1)

Theme: A manual of conduct
Date written: A.D. 62–64
Author: Paul
Setting: Macedonia

While on his way to Rome for his first imprisonment, Paul had briefly visited Crete, an island in the Mediterranean Sea. After his release, Paul returns to Crete for ministry and leaves Titus there. He is to continue the work that Paul started while Paul goes on to Macedonia. Titus is a trusted and longtime disciple of Paul's who served with Paul on his second and third missionary journeys. Paul now writes to Titus in response to a letter from Titus or a report that comes to him from Crete. Paul gives personal encouragement and counsel to a young pastor who is facing opposition from ungodly men within the newly formed churches. He gives instruction on how those young-in-the-faith believers are to conduct themselves before a pagan society that is eager to criticize this new religion and its people.

The Skeleton

▸ **Chapter 1** *The Qualifications of Church Leaders*

Paul opens with a brief greeting and then gives the first of three instructive statements: God purposed to save and build up the elect by His Word and ultimately bring them to eternal glory (Titus 1:1-4).

Paul goes on to inform Titus of one of his major duties—that of appointing qualified leaders in the churches on Crete. These leaders are to refute false teachers and to encourage the people in the church to live godly lives before their notoriously pagan neighbors.

▸ **Chapter 2** *The Conduct of Church Members*

Paul instructs Titus to speak sound words of truth to men and women, different age groups, and slaves so that they show a pattern of good works and gain credibility before the unbelieving world. Then Paul gives his second instructive statement touching on the basis for righteous living: Jesus Christ, through whom we receive God's gracious gift of salvation, redeems us so that we may be His special people—a people who are zealous to do good works (Titus 2:11-14). Paul urges Titus to proclaim these truths with authority.

▸ **Chapter 3** *The Conduct of Believers in General*

Titus is to remind the church members of their responsibilities in society—to be subject to rulers; to obey God and be ready for every good work; to speak no evil; and to be peaceable, gentle, and show all humility to all men. Paul then gives his third instructive statement: He reminds his readers that they were all once foolish and disobedient, yet God their Savior still came to bring salvation to them not on the basis of their works but His mercy. They have been made heirs of eternal life, having been justified by His grace (Titus 3:4-7).

Paul next exhorts Titus to deal firmly with dissenters who cause division and controversies. He closes his letter by asking Titus to come to him. Paul then gives a final challenge to the people to continue to be involved in good works and not be unfruitful.

Putting Meat on the Bones

The book of Titus is important because it stresses the need for righteous living among Christians as a testimony to the godless societies around them. The problem of immorality among the Cretans was not much different than the immorality found in other cities where Christianity was taking root. Paul writes Titus about equipping the people in the churches to live as effective witnesses for Jesus Christ.

Fleshing It Out in Your Life

Whether it's A.D. 62 or today, the corporate witness of a church must have a unified message. There cannot be dissension and strife. Sound teaching at all levels will help keep the church unified before the world. Equally important is godly behavior outside the church as you come in contact with unbelievers. Have you recently thought about your conduct both inside and outside the church? Ask God to give you insight into your behavior at church, and in public. May your godly behavior help promote unity within your church, and may your good works outside the church be a beacon light leading others to the Savior.

Life Lessons from Titus

- Spiritual leadership starts with what you are before it moves to what you are to do.
- Your conduct exposes your true spiritual condition.
- Your conduct is essential in your witness.
- Each age group and gender in the church has specific roles and responsibilities that, when fulfilled, reflect positively on God and His Word.

Where to Find It

God's election of believers . . . . Titus 1:1-2
Christ's deity . . . . .Titus 2:13
Christ's death for sinners . . . . Titus 2:14
A Christian's duty to obey the government . . . . .Titus 3:1
The Holy Spirt's ministry . . . . .Titus 3:5

The Ministry of Good Works

Christians are to be a pattern of good works	Titus 2:7
Christians are to be zealous for good works	Titus 2:14
Christians are to be ready for every good work	Titus 3:1
Christians are to be careful to maintain good works	Titus 3:8

Philemon

Perhaps [Onesimus] departed for a while for this pupose, that you might receive him forever, no longer as a slave but more than a slave— a beloved brother....
(Verses 15-16)

Theme: Forgiveness
Date written: A.D. 60–62
Author: Paul
Setting: Prison

A runaway slave from Colosse by the name of Onesimus makes his way to Rome and, in God's providence, becomes a Christian under Paul's ministry. Amazingly his master and owner, Philemon, had also been saved under Paul's ministry several years earlier (probably in Ephesus, which is not many miles from Colosse). Now Paul, a prisoner, wants to do the culturally right thing and send Onesimus, his new friend and fellow believer, back to his master, Philemon. Paul writes this letter beseeching his "beloved friend and fellow laborer" (verse 1) Philemon to forgive his runaway slave and receive him back as a new brother in Christ.

The Skeleton

▸ **Verses 1–3** *A Greeting from a Good Friend*

Paul normally dictated his letters, but because of the unusual nature of this letter, he decides to write it personally. He addresses it to Philemon, a Christian leader in Colosse, but also names Philemon's wife, Apphia, and their son, Archippus, in the letter, and even the entire church that meets in their home. They are all his beloved friends.

▸ **Verses 4-7** *The Character of One Who Forgives*

Paul thanks God for Philemon's love and faithfulness not only toward Jesus Christ, but also toward all the believers in Colosse, who have been refreshed by Philemon's ministry. Paul's commendation of Philemon is honest and heartfelt.

▸ **Verses 8-18** *The Actions of One Who Forgives*

Paul bases the appeal he is about to make on Philemon's character, rather than commanding Philemon to pardon and receive Onesimus. Paul doesn't use Onesimus' name until he is able to describe the dramatic change that has occurred in Onesimus' life. He tells Philemon that once Onesimus was of some use to Philemon. But now he is useful in his service to Paul, and he can also be useful in a similar way to Philemon. Paul pleads with Philemon to receive Onesimus back like he would receive Paul himself. Evidently Onesimus had stolen from his master, so Paul says Philemon is to put Onesimus' debt on his (Paul's) account.

▸ **Verses 19-25** *The Motive of One Who Forgives*

After Paul asks that Onesimus' debt be put on his account, Paul reminds Philemon of his greater spiritual debt as one of Paul's converts. Paul explains that this opportunity is a real test of Philemon's ability to forgive, and Paul expresses confidence in the outcome—that Onesimus may either be freed from slavery or given permission to engage in ministry—or both! Paul is hoping to be released from prison before long and asks that a room be prepared for his arrival.

Putting Meat on the Bones

The book of Philemon, along with the books of Ephesians, Philippians, and Colossians, are referred to as "prison epistles" because they were written while Paul was imprisoned for several years in Rome. In this shortest of the four prison epistles Paul tactfully appeals to his friend not to punish his runaway slave, Onesimus, but to forgive and restore him as a new Christian brother. This request would probably have been impossible to fulfill under normal circumstances. Slaves had a tough life, and those who had run away or stolen from their master—or, as in Onesimus' case, done both—would be in serious trouble. Philemon had every right under Roman law to punish or even kill Onesimus. But Christ's death has made forgiveness possible. In Christ, Philemon and anyone who names the name of Jesus can have the forgiveness of sins. Forgiveness is a very foundational aspect of Christianity.

Fleshing It Out in Your Life

On the basis of your forgiveness in Christ, you can and should be willing to forgive others. Your ability to forgive others is an indicator of the forgiveness you have received from God. Is there someone who has wronged you and, until now, you have been unwilling to forgive? Examine your heart. A forgiven Christian is a forgiving Christian.

Life Lessons from Philemon

- Coming to Christ does not relieve you of your past sinful actions.
- You are obligated to obey the law even though you might not personally agree with it.
- Forgiveness is most Christlike when it is given to the undeserving.
- Mediating on behalf of others is an important function of your Christian life.

Where to Find It

Paul's praise of Philemon . . . . Philemon 4-7
Paul's appeal to Philemon . . . . Philemon 8-14
Paul's vision for Onesimus . . . . Philemon 15-17
Paul's confidence in Philemon . . . . Philemon 18-21

Insights into the Ministry of the Apostle Paul

- He met the risen Lord Jesus Christ.
- He was a pioneer missionary and church planter.
- He was a discipler of men.
- He worked as a tentmaker to support his ministry.
- He began his formal ministry after the age of 40.
- He made his first missionary trip after the age of 45.
- He wrote his first epistle at the age of 49.
- He preached the gospel until he was put to death at about age 65.
- He wrote 13 God-inspired books of the New Testament.
- He was the most influential man in the New Testament other than Jesus Christ.

Hebrews

Seeing then that we have a great High Priest
who has passed through the heavens,
Jesus the Son of God,
let us hold fast our confession.
(4:14)

Theme: The superiority of Christ
Date written: A.D. 67–69
Author: Unknown
Setting: A community of Jewish Christians

Persecution is a real threat to the Jewish Christians in the newly forming churches of the first century. Many find themselves under intense persecution as they try to live out their newfound faith in Christ while living in Jewish communities where the Old Testament is the focus of religion. The unknown writer of the book of Hebrews believes that many Jewish Christians are in danger of slipping back into Judaism because of growing opposition. They need to mature and become stable in their faith. By demonstrating the superiority of Christ over all the Old Testament rituals and sacrifices, this unknown author exhorts these early believers to stay true to the gospel of Jesus Christ.

The Skeleton

▸ **Chapters 1–4:13** *Christ, a Superior Person*

Hebrews opens with the author showing that Christ is superior to the prophets who spoke forth God's revelation, and He is the ultimate revelation of God. The writer adds that even though angels are special beings, Christ is superior to the angels because He is God's Son. Christ is also superior to Moses, the great lawgiver, who was merely God's servant, whereas Christ is God's Son. And unlike Moses, Christ can lead His people into rest. Even though Joshua led the Israelites into their inheritance, there still remains a better rest for God's people in the future. Christ, from His superior position, will provide that final rest.

▸ **Chapters 4:14–10:18** *Christ's Superior Priesthood*

The priesthood is very important in Judaism, but Christ's priesthood is superior to even Aaron's priesthood. That is because Christ's priesthood comes from the order of Melchizedek, an Old Testament priest who blessed Abraham, the forefather of Levi and the Levitical priesthood, of which Aaron was the first priest. Christ's priesthood is the perfect fulfillment of this order of Melchizedek because it was established by an oath from God, is unaffected by death, and is unmarred by sin. No priest can be this qualified, therefore Christ's priesthood is superior. Christ has become a permanent and perfect High Priest and "the mediator of a better covenant" (8:6). This new covenant has made the old one obsolete. Similarly, our Great High Priest—the Lord Jesus Christ—ministers in a "greater and more perfect tabernacle not made with hands" (9:11). Also, Christ offers Himself as a sinless and voluntary sacrifice once and for all, whereas the old priesthood had to offer sacrifices continually.

▸ **Chapters 10:19–12:29** *Christ's Superior Faith*

The author sums up all he has been saying about Christ by warning his readers of the danger of discarding their superior faith, which is based on a superior Savior. The faith that the readers must maintain is defined and illustrated with the lives of many Old Testament believers such as Abraham, Sarah, David, Samuel, and others. The readers need to fix their eyes on Jesus, the author and perfecter of genuine faith, who endured great hostility on the cross. And those who believe in Him will sometimes have to endure difficulty and divine discipline for the sake of holiness.

▸ **Chapter 13** *Superior Christian Behavior*

This last chapter focuses on some of the essential practical ethics of Christian living. These ethics are to be shaped by the readers' dedication to Christ. This superior behavior will also be manifested in love, in a godly marriage, by a lack of covetousness, and in contentment and obedience. This kind of Christlike behavior helps portray the true gospel to the world, encouraging others to believe in Christ and thus bringing glory to God.

Putting Meat on the Bones

The Jewish religion was divinely designed and expressed true worship and devotion to God. The commandments, rituals, and the prophets described God's promises of the Messiah and revealed the way to forgiveness and salvation. But then Jesus Christ, the Messiah, came, fulfilling the law and the prophets, nullifying the need for sacrifices, conquering sin, and providing eternal life through His sacrificial death.

The message of Jesus was hard for the Jews to accept. Many were violently opposed to the gospel of Christ. Those who did accept Jesus as the Messiah often found themselves drifting back into their old and familiar religious ways, especially as persecution mounted. Hebrews was written to these people with the overarching message that Christianity is superior to the Jewish religion and every other religious system because Christ is superior and He is completely sufficient for salvation.

Fleshing It Out in Your Life

Faith is confident trust in God and the salvation He provides in His Son Jesus, who is the only one who can save you from sin. If you trust in Jesus Christ for your complete salvation, He will transform you completely. That transformation and subsequent growth enables you to face trials, stay true to God when you are being persecuted, and build your character. Don't allow persecution, temptation, or the lure of an inferior religious system to cause you to hesitate in your commitment to Jesus. Your Savior is superior, your faith placed in your Savior is superior, and your final victory through your Savior is assured.

Life Lessons from Hebrews

- The superiority of Christianity is based on the superiority of Christ.
- Salvation in Christ and freedom from sin are gifts from God, but you are given the responsibility to grow and strengthen your faith and trust in God.
- The process of maturing your faith in God takes time.
- Maturity keeps you from being easily swayed in your beliefs.
- You can have victory in your trials when you keep your eyes focused on Christ.

Where to Find It

The ministry of God's Word . . . . Hebrews 4:12-13
The king of Salem, Melchizedek . . . . Hebrews 7:1-22
God's definition of faith . . . . Hebrews 11:1
God's "hall of faith" . . . . Hebrews 11
The race of faith . . . . Hebrews 12:1
God's discipline of His children . . . . Hebrew 12:3-11

A Comparison of the Two Sacrifices

The sacrifices under the law were:	The sacrifice of Christ was:
A reminder of sin	The removal of sin
Offered continually	Offered once
The blood of animals	The blood of Christ
A covering for sin	The cleansing of sin
Involuntary	Voluntary

James

Faith by itself, if it does not
have works, is dead.
(2:17)

Theme: Genuine faith
Date written: A.D. 44–49
Author: James
Setting: Jerusalem

The book of James is the earliest of the New Testament epistles or letters. It was written by James, a resident of Jerusalem and a leader of the church there. The people in the Jerusalem church—the first church—had been scattered to a number of Roman provinces due to persecution. James feels compelled to exhort and encourage them in their struggles. Genuine faith, James explains, will produce real changes in a person's conduct and character. In a style similar to that of the Old Testament book of Proverbs, James presents a series of tests by which a person's faith in Christ can be measured. If real change is absent, then readers are to examine their faith to make sure they are not exhibiting symptoms of dead faith—which is really no faith!

The Skeleton

▸ **Chapters 1–2** *Actions of Faith*

James, the half-brother of Jesus, opens with a one-verse greeting to the Jewish Christians scattered everywhere. Then he immediately begins sharing how genuine faith is proved and strengthened by the outward test of trials. James explains that trials are designed to produce maturity, endurance, and dependence upon God as a believer turns to Him for wisdom and enablement. Regarding temptation, James explains:

- ▸ Temptations are inward tests of faith
- ▸ Temptations do not come from God
- ▸ Temptations are handled by responding and becoming doers and not mere hearers of the word.

James goes on to analyze the concept of Christian faith by explaining that true faith does not show partiality to the rich over the poor. True faith will "love your neighbor as yourself" (2:8). James concludes by mentioning Abraham and Rahab from the Old Testament as perfect examples of those whose faith was demonstrated by their actions.

▸ **Chapter 3** *Evaluation of Faith*

James refers to the tongue as another test of how true faith acts—faith tames the tongue. He goes on to cite wisdom as a further evidence of faith. Just as you can identify a tree by the type of fruit it produces, you can evaluate the kind of wisdom a person possesses by his or her actions. James also distinguishes between ***human*** wisdom, which leads to disorder, and *God's* wisdom, which leads to peace and goodness.

▸ **Chapters 4:1–5:6** *Conflicts of Faith*

Worldliness is a detriment to faith. It produces covetousness, envy, fighting, and pride. The only thing that can help overcome worldliness is submission to God with a humble and repentant heart. This attitude of submission will transform one's actions. A for-real Christian will not complain, nor presume on God. Instead, he or she will submit their life and plans into His hands. This spirit of humility will guard a believer in Christ from seeking to accrue wealth...which could lead one right back into pride and selfishness.

▸ **Chapter 5:7-20** *Forbearance of Faith*

James ends by asking his readers to be patient as they endure suffering, and to take comfort in knowing that someday, the Lord will return. They are to follow the examples of the prophets, and men like Job, who suffered with patience. In all such cases, the Lord was compassionate and merciful. Therefore, James's readers are to pray in the midst of their suffering and sickness, being confident that the prayers of the righteous—those with true faith (like that of the prophet Elijah)—

will have a beneficial effect. James closes by challenging his readers to pursue those who stray from biblical truth and are not living according to God's principles because their souls are in danger of eternal separation from God.

Putting Meat on the Bones

Christians are often guilty of harming their witness through their actions. Professing to trust God and be His people and yet continuing to hold tightly to the world and its values is a contradiction. Claiming to have true faith and appearing to possess all the right answers while still pursuing wealth and worldly pleasures can have a detrimental effect on how unbelievers perceive the gospel message.

Fleshing It Out in Your Life

James is a reminder that genuine faith transforms lives. You must put your faith in Christ into action. It is easy to say you have faith, but true faith will produce loving actions toward others. Your faith must not be mere head knowledge, but it must also be lived out by heart actions. The proof that your faith is genuine is a changed life manifested by practical Christian living. James 1:19 says believers are to be "swift to hear, slow to speak, slow to wrath." You cannot get much more practical than that!

Life Lessons from James

- Genuine faith will produce real changes in your life.
- Temptation is not sin, but if it is not dealt with, it can lead to sin.
- Being wealthy is not a sin, but selfishness is. God gives you money to help meet the needs of others.
- Prayer plays a significant role in the ministry of the local church.
- God is not a respecter of persons, and you should not be either.

Where to Find It

The benefits of trials . . . . James 1:2-4
The solution to a lack of wisdom . . . . James 1:5-8
The nature of temptation . . . . James 1:12-15
The fact that faith without works is dead . . . . James 2:17
The untamable tongue . . . . James 3:1-12

The Divine Nature of God: God Is...

The giver of wisdom (1:5)

Not tempted by evil (1:13)

The giver of every good gift (1:17)

Unchanging (1:17)

The Father of lights—the Creator (1:17-18)

The Righteous One (1:20)

Our Father (3:9)

The giver of grace to the humble (4:6)

The lawgiver (4:12)

The sovereign Lord (4:15)

1 Peter

For to this you were called,
because Christ also suffered for us,
leaving us an example,
that you should follow His steps.
(2:21)

Theme: Responding to suffering
Date written: A.D. 64–65
Author: Peter
Setting: Rome

First Peter was written around the time Rome was burned by the emperor, Nero. The persecution of Christians had been steadily increasing, and its intensity will only accelerate as Nero spreads the false rumor that the fires were started by Christians. Peter writes this letter to Christians throughout the Roman Empire to show them how to live victoriously in the midst of the coming hostility without losing hope, without becoming resentful, and by trusting the Lord and looking for His second coming. Peter believes that if his readers will live obediently in the midst of a hostile society, they can be evangelistic tools in the hand of God.

The Skeleton

▸ **Chapters 1:1–2:10** *Recounting God's Great Salvation*

Addressing his letter to believers in several Roman provinces, Peter begins by thanking God for the gift of salvation. Then Peter explains to his readers that trials will refine their faith. In spite of their circumstances, they should believe in God's plan of salvation, just as many in the past believed. Even the prophets of old who wrote about it believed it, even though they did not understand it. But now salvation has been revealed in Christ. So, in response to such a great salvation, Peter exhorts his readers to live holy lives, to reverently fear and trust God, to be honest and loving in their relationships with others, and to become like living stones with Christ, the "precious" and "chief cornerstone" upon which the church is to be built (2:4,6).

▸ **Chapters 2:11–4:6** *Recalling Christ's Example*

Peter next explains how believers should live in the world during difficult times. They should be above reproach, imitating Christ in all their social roles, whether as masters or slaves, husbands or wives, younger or older, church members or neighbors. Peter desires that if suffering is to come, it won't be for evil activity, but for godly behavior. He points his readers to Jesus Christ as their example for obedience to God in the midst of great suffering.

▸ **Chapter 4:7-19** *Rejoicing in the Lord's Return*

Peter warns that the end is at hand and the Lord's return is near. Therefore, Chrsitians need to be serious and watchful in their prayers, to love one another, be hospitable, use their spiritual gifts to serve each other, and rejoice in their suffering—all of which brings glory to God.

▸ **Chapter 5** *Revealing Some Special Instructions*

Peter gives these final words of instruction: Elders are to shepherd their people; younger people are to submit to the leadership of the elders; and all are to be submissive to each other in humility. In humility, believers are to put their cares into God's hands because God cares for them. Believers are also to resist the devil as he walks about like a roaring lion. Finally, Peter concludes with a great statement of assurance: God is working through all that is going on in the lives of his readers—even their struggles—to produce strength of character, which will also bring glory to God.

Putting Meat on the Bones

Peter composed this letter to Christians who were experiencing persecution because of their faith in Christ. He wrote to comfort them by reminding them of their salvation and the hope of eternal life. He challenged them to live holy lives and to realize that those who suffer for their faith become partners with Christ in His suffering.

Fleshing It Out in Your Life

Today, many Christians around the world are suffering for what they believe. You may or may not be among them. But all Christians should expect persecution, for Jesus said, "In the world you will have tribulation" (John 16:33). If your faith is seen by others, you can expect some ridicule and rejection. But Peter says you don't have to be terrified by such treatment. Though you live in this world with its persecution, you are also a citizen of heaven who will live in eternity with Christ. This dual citizenship should give you confidence and hope to stand firm whenever your faith in Christ is challenged. You need to see each confrontation as an opportunity to have your faith refined and strengthened. As you face persecution and suffering, remember Peter's words: "For to this you were called, because Christ also suffered for us, leaving us an example, that you should follow His steps" (1 Peter 2:21).

Life Lessons from 1 Peter

- You are expected to submit to governing authorities.
- Your conduct should point unbelievers to Christ, especially those in your family.
- You should not be surprised when persecution comes.
- You can face persecution victoriously as Christ did if you rely on Christ for strength.

Where to Find It

Desire for the pure milk of God's Word . . . . 1 Peter 2:1-2
Submission to governments . . . . 1 Peter 2:13-17
Submission of wives . . . . 1 Peter 3:1-6

Responsibility of husbands . . . . 1 Peter 3:7
Teaching about spiritual gifts . . . . 1 Peter 4:10-11
Responsibility of elders . . . . 1 Peter 5:1-4
Devil pictured as a roaring lion . . . . 1 Peter 5:8

The Man Called Peter

- Was a fisherman by occupation
- Was one of the first to be called to serve with Jesus
- Was one of the 12 disciples
- Was one of the inner group of three disciples, along with James and John
- Was brash and impulsive in speech and actions
- Denied Christ three times
- Was restored by Christ to "feed" His sheep—His people
- Preached the first sermon after the founding of the church
- Had difficulty with receiving Gentiles into the church
- Supplied John Mark with eyewitness accounts of the life of Jesus
- Wrote 1 and 2 Peter
- Was, according to tradition, crucified upside down in Rome

2 Peter

We have the prophetic word confirmed, which you do well to heed as a light that shines in a dark place, until the day dawns and the morning star rises in your hearts....
(1:19)

Theme: Warning against false teachers
Date written: A.D. 67–68
Author: Peter
Setting: A Roman prison

About three years after he wrote his first letter, the apostle Peter writes a second one, in which he expresses alarm about the false teachers who have invaded the churches in Asia Minor. They have already caused many problems, and Peter foresees that their false teachings and immoral lifestyles will continue to have a disastrous effect on the churches they have infiltrated. Therefore, as a last will and testament, Peter writes this letter from his prison cell to warn believers about the dangers of false teachers. To be prepared for what's coming, his readers need to know a few things.

The Skeleton

▸ **Chapter 1** *Know the Bible*

After a brief introduction, Peter says that the cure for stagnation and shortsightedness in the Christian life is the knowledge of truth. His readers need to continue to develop their Christian character, which will give them assurance of their salvation. He explains that his days are numbered and that his readers need to heed his warning and listen to his apostolic message and the words of Scripture.

▸ **Chapter 2** *Know the Enemy*

Peter next gives a very graphic description of the false teachers who are becoming prevalent in these last days. They will do or say anything for money. They laugh at the things of God. They do what they feel like doing. They are proud and boastful. Their crafty words are capable of enticing immature believers. But God will deliver His people and punish those who seek to destroy their faith.

▸ **Chapter 3** *Know the Future*

Peter now tells his readers that in both his first and this present second letter he is reminding them of what they can expect from false teachers. They scoff at the idea of Christ's second coming, and they claim that God does not intervene in world affairs. But Peter calls attention to three divine interventions: creation, the flood, and the coming destruction of the heavens and the earth. He explains that what seems like an unfulfilled promise on God's part is due to His patience in waiting for more people to come to a saving knowledge of Christ. Nevertheless, the day of the Lord *will* come, and God *will* establish a new heaven and earth. In light of this coming day of the Lord, Peter exhorts his readers to lives of holiness, steadfastness, and growth.

Putting Meat on the Bones

Previously Peter had written to comfort and encourage believers who were in the midst of persecution and suffering—that is, external attacks by the enemy of their souls. Now three years later he is writing to warn the churches of internal attacks through stagnation and heresy. In Peter's mind, the cure for these two problems is growth in the grace and knowledge of Christ. The best antidote for error is a maturing understanding of the truth. This growth comes from the Word of God, which contains everything a believer needs for "life and godliness" (1:3).

Fleshing It Out in Your Life

Warnings come in many forms—lights, signs, sounds, smells, and the written word. No one who values their physical life would fail to respond to one or all of these forms of warning. Are you reading God's warnings of spiritual danger found in the Bible? And are you responding to them? Don't turn your back on God's warnings. Heed 2 Peter 3:18 and grow in the grace and knowledge of Jesus. Spiritual growth will keep you faithful and give you the discernment to defend against the wiles and ways of Satan and his false teachers.

Life Lessons from 2 Peter

- You are commanded to grow in your knowledge of God.
- Your growth combats spiritual laziness and deception by the enemy.
- Do not fail to heed the warnings of Scripture.
- Each day that the Lord delays His return is to be a day devoted to holy living and diligent service.

Where to Find It

Our sufficiency in Christ . . . . 2 Peter 1:2-3
The origin of Scripture . . . . 2 Peter 1:20-21
A brief history of God's judgment . . . . 2 Peter 2:4-11
God's view of time . . . . .2 Peter 3:8

The Day of the Lord

2 Peter 3:10-13

It will be a day of punishment for ungodly men.

It will come like a thief in the night.

The heavens will be dissolved.

The earth will be burned up with fire.

A new heaven and a new earth will be created.

1 John

That which we have seen and
heard we declare to you,
that you also may have fellowship with us;
and truly our fellowship is with the Father
and with His Son Jesus Christ.
(1:3)

Theme: Fellowship with God
Date written: A.D. 90
Author: John
Setting: Ephesus

Although advanced in age and probably the sole surviving apostle and original disciple of Christ, John continues to be actively involved in ministry. As the last remaining apostle, his words are highly authoritative among the churches of Asia Minor. In this letter (as well as in 2 and 3 John) he writes to these churches with a pastor's heart. It has been some 50 years since Jesus physically walked the earth. Most of the eyewitnesses of Christ's ministry had died by now, but John was still alive to testify about Jesus. He had walked and talked with Jesus, had seen Him heal the sick and raise the dead, had watched Him die, and had witnessed His resurrection and ascension to heaven. John *knew* God—he had experienced fellowship with Him and watched Him teach, serve, and minister to others. Now, out of concern for a new generation of believers, John wants his readers to know they have assurance of the indwelling God through their abiding relationship with Christ. In simple terms, he describes what it means to have fellowship with God. At the same time, he warns that false teachers have entered the churches, denying that Jesus had actually come in the flesh. They openly reject the incarnation of Christ, and John writes from personal experience to correct this error.

The Skeleton

▸ **Chapters 1:1–2:2** *The Basis of Fellowship*

John opens his letter by giving his credentials as an eyewitness to the person of Christ. Jesus was not merely a spirit, but one who could be physically touched. John's purpose is to transmit his personal witness of Christ's life and ministry to his readers so they may share in the same sweet fellowship John enjoyed with Jesus Christ. This fellowship is made possible by the blood of Jesus, which cleanses the believer and satisfies the Father's righteous demands against sin. As a result, believers will walk in this light of God's fellowship and willingly confess sin, knowing that they have an advocate with the Father, Jesus Christ.

▸ **Chapter 2:3-27** *The Companions of Fellowship*

Fellowship with God has actions that are associated with it. These actions are the constant companion of a believer. One who abides with God will live in obedience, walk in Christlikeness, love his brother, separate from the world, confess Jesus as the Son of God, and have the anointing of the Holy Spirit.

▸ **Chapters 2:28–3:23** *The Mark of Fellowship*

The basic theme of 1 John is summarized: Fellowship with Christ comes through a close relationship with Him. This happens when a person is regenerated—born again. One in fellowship with Christ practices righteousness, anticipates His appearing, has an aversion to sin, and loves the family of God (as opposed to Cain's murder of his brother, Abel). A believer's love is manifested in self-sacrifice and gives one assurance before God.

▸ **Chapters 3:24–4:21** *The Proof of Fellowship*

John now introduces the important concept of the indwelling of believers by God, the Holy Spirit. The Spirit of God residing in a person confesses that Jesus has come in the flesh and manifests love for others.

This love affirms the reality of Jesus—God in flesh—and anticipates the perfect fellowship to come. This love gives a believer confidence to one day meet the one from whom all love is derived, Jesus.

▸ **Chapter 5** *The Assurance of Fellowship*

John concludes by listing a number of ways believers can be assured of their fellowship with God. They will: 1) believe in Jesus Christ; 2) have love for both the Father and the Son; 3) keep God's commandments; 4) experience victory over the world; 5) experience the witness of the Holy Spirit; 6) possess eternal life; and 7) be assured of answered prayer.

Putting Meat on the Bones

Many wonder about the true identity of Jesus. Was He just a good man—maybe one of the best who ever lived? Was He a man with illusions of grandeur—a man with a Messiah complex? Was He really the God-man, 100 percent God and 100 percent man? Hearing such speculations about Jesus could possibly cause a person to wonder or even doubt. John rushes to reassure his readers with a set of fundamentals of the Christian faith. Basic to the Christian faith is that Jesus alone is qualified to offer up the perfect sacrifice for our sins—His body. He and He alone is capable of satisfying God the Father's requirement for the payment of the debt of sin.

Fleshing It Out in Your Life

John is writing this letter to dispel any doubts believers might have and to give assurance that, if you believe in the Son of God, you have eternal life. John does this by painting a clear picture of Jesus, the Christ, the Son of God, God in flesh. Do you yet believe in the Son of God? If you do, John says, "This is the testimony: that God has given us eternal life, and this life is in His Son. He who has the Son has life" (1 John 5:11–12). Armed with this testimony of your fellowship with God, you are to live in holiness, love your fellow believers, and long for His reappearing in glory.

Life Lessons from 1 John

- Love is a mark of your fellowship with God.
- You are commanded to love others as Jesus did.
- You must resist sin, and when you do sin, you must confess your wrong to God.
- Fellowship with God is a promise, but it is also a responsibility for how you are to live your life.

Where to Find It

The spirit of Antichrist . . . . 1 John 4:1–3
"Perfect love casts out fear" . . . . 1 John 4:18
The criterion for eternal life . . . . 1 John 5:12

Facts about John, the Disciple Whom Jesus Loved

John 21:20

- A fisherman by occupation
- One of John the Baptist's followers before following Jesus
- One of the three disciples closest to Jesus, along with his brother, James, and Peter (Matthew 17:1; 26:37)
- Nicknamed by Jesus, along with his brother, James, as the "Sons of Thunder" (Mark 3:17)
- Asked for a special position in Jesus' kingdom
- Leaned on Jesus' breast during the last supper
- Ministered with Peter (Acts 3:1; 4:13; 8:14)
- Became a "pillar" in the Jerusalem church (Galatians 2:9)
- Exiled to the island of Patmos (Revelation 1:9)
- Longest-living disciple
- Wrote five New Testament books (the Gospel of John; 1, 2, 3 John; Revelation)

2 John

If anyone comes to you and does not bring this doctrine [of Christ], do not receive him into your house nor greet him; for he who greets him shares in his evil deeds.
(Verses 10-11)

Theme: Christian discernment
Date written: A.D. 90–95
Author: John
Setting: Ephesus

The apostle John is still dealing with the same problem he addressed in his first epistle—that of false teachers. In this second letter John is concerned with the itinerant ministry false teachers are conducting as they seek to make converts in the different churches that are under John's authority. John is writing to a specific woman who may have unknowingly or unwisely shown hospitality to these false teachers. John fears they may be taking advantage of her kindness, and warns her not to show hospitality to any of these deceivers.

The Skeleton

▸ **Verses 1-3** *The Greeting*

John calls himself "the Elder" as he sends greetings to an unknown "elect lady" and her children. As in all his writings, John describes a Christian's relationship with God as living in truth and love.

▸ **Verses 4-6** *The Commendation*

The apostle commends his readers for their walk in obedience to God. He reminds them that this commandment to be hospitable entails the practice of love for one another.

▸ **Verses 7-11** *The Warning*

John now admonishes his readers to watch out for deceivers who do not affirm that Jesus Christ actually came in the flesh. They are "antichrists," he explains, so do not in any way show hospitality to them. Do not even give them a greeting and thus share in their evil deeds.

▸ **Verses 12-13** *The Blessing*

John closes this brief letter saying he has more to say but will wait until he comes to them to share his further thoughts so that their joy may be full.

Putting Meat on the Bones

John has seen truth and love firsthand—he has been with Jesus. So affected is he with these ideals that all his writings—the Gospel of John, 1 John, and now 2 John—are filled with these themes. Truth and love are vital to the Christian and inseparable in a Christian's life. In this short letter to a dear friend, John advises her to follow the truth, love God, and show hospitality to those who adhere to the fundamentals of the faith. At the same time, she is to avoid those who are attempting to destroy these basic beliefs.

Fleshing It Out in Your Life

John's concern is appropriate today as well. Your Christian hospitality is to be practiced with discernment. You are not called to automatically accept anyone who claims to be a believer. Accepting a false teacher into your home can actually aid those who are attempting to destroy the very beliefs you hold so dear and which so many have paid such a high price to preserve. How are you to discern truth from error? First, read and study God's Word. Next, compare what others are teaching with what the Bible says. And then avoid those who don't abide in the teachings of Christ.

Life Lessons from 2 John

- Walking in obedience to the truth is to be a continual habit in your life.
- Be careful! False teachers are very deceptive. Look at their lives and their message to see if they match with Scripture.
- Avoiding hospitality is reserved only for those who would destroy the truth of Christ.
- Disagreement over minor issues is not a reason for avoiding hospitality.

Where to Find It

Greetings to "the elect lady" . . . . Verse 1
Walking in the truth . . . . Verse 4
Walking in God's commandments . . . . Verse 6
Definition of a deceiver and an Antichrist . . . . Verse 7
Admonition not to receive those who deny Christ into your home . . . . Verse 10

Some Who Showed Hospitality in the Bible

Abraham to three angelic beings	Genesis 18:1-8
Lot to two angels	Genesis 19:1-11
Laban to Abraham's servant	Genesis 24:11-61
The Shunammite woman to Elijah	2 Kings 4:8-10
Mary and Martha to Jesus and His disciples	Luke 10:38-42
Priscilla and Aquila to Paul	Acts 18:2
The New Testament widows	1 Timothy 5:9-10

3 John

Beloved, you do faithfully whatever you do
for the brethren and for strangers.
(Verse 5)

Theme: Christian hospitality
Date written: A.D. 90–95
Author: John
Setting: Ephesus

This is John's third letter written to those under his care and leadership. As with 2 John, this letter deals with Christian hospitality. In John's day, church leaders traveled from town to town helping to establish new churches and strengthen existing ones. These church workers depended on the hospitality of fellow believers. This letter includes three different messages about three men: John commends Gaius for his ministry of hospitality; he condemns the self-serving ministry of Diotrephes; and he congratulates Demetrius for his good testimony.

The Skeleton

▸ **Verses 1-8** *Gaius's Hospitality*

Again, John calls himself "the Elder" as he responds with joy to a report that his "beloved Gaius" is walking in the truth. John acknowledges his actions toward traveling teachers and missionaries. These travelers accept no funds from unbelievers and depend entirely upon the hospitality of faithful Christians such as Gaius. John encourages Gaius to continue to participate in their ministries.

▸ **Verses 9-10** *Diotrephes's Lack of Hospitality*

John now shifts to a negative example in a man named Diotrephes, whose pride won't allow him to accept these itinerant teachers sent out by the apostle. If anyone in the church tries to accept one of these teachers, Diotrephes has him removed from the church. John anticipates the need to exercise his authority and confront Diotrephes for his un-Christian-like conduct.

▸ **Verses 11-13** *Demetrius's Good Testimony*

John cautions his readers to not imitate what is evil (such as the conduct of Diotrephes in verses 9-10, whose beliefs are not in question, but whose application of those beliefs is). Diotrephes's evil actions show a blindness to the very thing John has preached passionately about in his first two letters—we are to love one another. On the other hand, Demetrius's life is a testimony of what is good. He is highly spoken of by all, including John himself, and even his very life is a living reality of the truth.

Putting Meat on the Bones

Love, humility, and a knowledge of the truth are essential to biblical hospitality. Gaius showed perfect hospitality and welcomed those who believed and taught the truth. Diotrephes's pride would not allow him to show hospitality to those who needed it, merited it, and could have benefited from it in his church. Demetrius was another who did what was right in the area of "stranger love"—showing hospitality to believers in need.

Fleshing It Out in Your Life

Third John is a great reminder of the constructive role of hospitality in the church...and the destructive power of pride in a church leader. Whether you are a leader or a member in your church, "be hospitable to one another without grumbling" (1 Peter 4:9). Be discerning of those whom you welcome into your home. Be faithful to extend hospitality as a ministry. Be careful not to let pride interfere in God's command to receive and care for others. Be sure to show love one to another.

Life Lessons from 3 John

- Strive to walk in the truth. It will ensure a spirit of loving hospitality.
- Realize Christian teachers, leaders, and missionaries need your support.
- Partner with Christian workers in their ministries by supporting them.
- Encourage Christian workers so they don't grow weary in their service.
- Be careful not to misuse any leadership position.

Where to Find It

Blessings of health and prosperity of soul . . . . .Verse 2
Joy due to the truth in others . . . . .Verse 3
Joy in knowing your "children" walk in truth . . . . .Verse 4
Reasons for helping Christian workers . . . . Verses 5-8
Warning against desiring preeminence . . . . .Verse 9
Command to imitate what is good, and not what is evil. . . . . .Verse 11

The Apostles James and John

- James and John were brothers.
- James was the older brother.
- James and John were fishermen from Galilee.
- James and John were the sons of Zebedee.
- Jesus called them "Sons of Thunder" (Mark 3:17).
- John was one of the three most intimate associates of Jesus.
- John identified himself as "the disciple whom Jesus loved" (John 21:20).
- John is sometimes referred to as "the apostle of love."
- John was exiled late in life to the island of Patmos, where he wrote the book of Revelation.
- James was the first apostle to be martyred.
- John's manner of death is unknown.

Jude

Beloved, while I was very diligent to write to you concerning our common salvation, I found it necessary to write to you exhorting you to contend earnestly for the faith....
(Verse 3)

Theme: Contending for the faith
Date written: A.D. 68–69
Author: Jude
Setting: Jerusalem

Although Jude had earlier rejected Jesus as the Messiah, he, along with his other three half-brothers of Jesus, was converted after Christ's resurrection. Because of his close family relationship with Jesus and because he was an eyewitness of Jesus' life, ministry, and resurrection, Jude has a burning passion for the salvation that comes in Christ. But as he writes, he transitions to a matter that is heavy on his heart at this time. Jude is intensely concerned about the threat of heretical teachers in the church and the response that Christians should have concerning this threat. Therefore, Jude seeks to motivate his readers to wake up from their complacency and take action against false teachers.

The Skeleton

▸ **Verses 1-4** *The Reason for Writing*

Jude begins by identifying himself as a "bondservant" of Jesus and as the brother of James, whom history and Scripture tell us was the leader of the Jerusalem church, the author of the book of James, and the half-brother of Jesus. Jude is about to write a treatise on salvation when grim news forces him to put aside this topic. In light of those who are denying Christ and using the grace of God to justify immoral behavior, Jude writes this timely word of rebuke and warning.

▸ **Verses 5-16** *The Danger of False Teachers*

Jude begins this section by reminding his readers that false teachers will meet their doom just as three other groups in the Old Testament met theirs: Contentious unbelievers who died in the wilderness; fallen angels who cohabited with women before the flood and who are in chains until judgment; and men who exhibited homosexual behavior and were destroyed in the destruction of Sodom and Gomorrah. False teachers are characterized by Jude as being ruled by their flesh, rejecting authority, and reviling angelic beings. Jude compares false teachers to three spiritually rebellious men in the Bible—Cain (from Genesis), and Korah and Balaam (from Numbers)—and says their evil is likened to hidden reefs, airy clouds, uprooted trees, wild waves, and wandering stars. Jude affirms the judgment of God upon these ungodly men.

▸ **Verses 17-25** *The Duty to Fight for God's Truth*

After exposing the behavior of false teachers, Jude now addresses his readers and reminds them that others have warned about these men. He exhorts them to protect themselves against this onslaught of apostasy by building themselves up in the Scriptures, praying consistently in the Spirit for God's will, and looking for Christ's second coming. In the process of fighting for God's truth, they are to show compassion to those who deserve it and, if necessary, to pull others out of the fires of apostasy with great fear of personal defilement. Jude then returns to the theme of salvation that he mentioned at the beginning of his letter. He closes with one of the most often-cited doxologies in the Bible (verses 24-25), emphasizing the power of Christ to preserve His followers from being overpowered by the enemy.

Putting Meat on the Bones

It is a human characteristic to fight for survival and to defend that which is most precious—home, family, and freedom. God's truths as found in the Bible are of infinite value, and they are under attack. Through the centuries many have opposed God's people and the truth they represent. These enemies of God twist the truth, seeking to deceive and destroy the unsuspecting. But God's truths and His Word still stand, being carried and defended by those who have committed their lives to Jesus Christ. It is an important responsibility and a great privilege to be a part of this great heritage.

Fleshing It Out in Your Life

What value do you place on God's Word? God's church? God's people? Today, as in years gone by, many false teachers have infiltrated our churches, Bible colleges, and Christian institutions. What price are you willing to pay to defend God's truth? Are you ready to stand with Jude and "contend earnestly for the faith which was once for all delivered to the saints" (verse 3)? If so, then you stand with Jude in the long line of faithful Christian soldiers who have answered the call and are fighting the good fight of faith as they engage the forces of evil for the souls of men.

Life Lessons from Jude

- As long as Satan is alive and well, false teachers will threaten the church with error. Do what you must to know the truth.
- Mark it well: One of the revealing characteristics of a false teacher is his fearless, ungodly behavior.
- False teachers act as if God will not punish their godless behavior.
- Genuine servants of God will faithfully point to Christ with their words and their conduct.
- Complacency is not an option for Christians. You are to earnestly contend for the faith.

Where to Find It

Warning from Jude of the fact of apostasy . . . . .Verse 4
Description of Michael, the archangel . . . . .Verse 9

Warnings from the apostles of the fact of apostasy . . . . .Verse 18
Blessings of knowing and following God .Verse 24
Blessing of the all-wise God, our Savior .Verse 25

Jude's Description of an Apostate

Godless (verse 4)
Immoral (verse 4)
Denies Christ (verse 4)
Rebels against authority (verse 8)
A grumbler (verse 16)
A fault finder (verse 16)
Mocks the truth (verse 18)
Divisive (verse 19)
Worldly (verse 19)
Lacks the Holy Spirit (verse 19)

Revelation

The Revelation of Jesus Christ,
which God gave Him to show His servants—
things which must shortly take place.
And He sent and signified it by His angel
to His servant John.
(1:1)

Theme: The unveiling of Jesus Christ
Date written: A.D. 94–96
Author: John
Setting: Isle of Patmos

By this time, John is the sole survivor of the original 12 disciples. Now an elderly man, he has been banished to Patmos, a small island in the Aegean Sea off the coast of Ephesus, for his faithful preaching of the gospel. While on Patmos, John receives a series of visions that describe the future history of the world. The visions reveal Jesus Christ as the divine Shepherd who is concerned about the condition of the church, as the righteous Judge who will punish the wicked, and as the triumphant King who will establish His kingdom for all eternity.

The Skeleton

▸ **Chapter 1** *The Vision of the Glorified Christ*

The apostle John is told to write about "the things which you have seen, and the things which are, and the things which will take place after this" (verse 19). John sees the glorified Christ and describes Him in a way similar to the visions of God in the Old Testament (see Daniel and

Ezekiel). Jesus is seen moving among His churches with a desire that His people be pure and free of sin. In a common response to seeing the awesome glory of the Lord, John falls at Jesus' feet in fear and dread.

▸ **Chapters 2–3** *The Letters to the Seven Churches*

In John's vision, Jesus speaks to seven different churches that are in various states of spiritual health. Most of the churches receive both praise for their good deeds and rebuke for the problems in their midst. Christ commends those who take a stand for truth and are willing to suffer for Him and condemns those who have lost their love for Him, tolerated the presence of sin, or become enamored by worldly riches.

▸ **Chapters 4–5** *The Scene in Heaven*

Chapter 4 opens with a scene in heaven, where John sees God upon His throne surrounded by many who worship Him day and night without ceasing. One of the songs of worship declares, "You are worthy, O Lord, to receive glory and honor and power; for You created all things, and by Your will they exist and were created" (4:11). Chapter 5 continues the worship of the Holy Lamb by angels, elders, and living creatures. In addition, Christ, the only One worthy, opens seven seals signifying God's unfolding punishments and judgments upon the earth.

▸ **Chapters 6–20** *The Pouring Out of Judgment*

John reveals what will take place during the last days, or the seven-year Tribulation. Jesus opens the first of the "seven seals" on a scroll, thus beginning the destruction. Then come the "seven trumpets" followed by the "seven bowls." These judgments describe the series of judgments in which God pours out His wrath upon the earth. Yet even in this time of judgment, God's mercy shines as brightly as ever as He continues to use various means to reach the lost with the message of salvation through Jesus Christ. During this time the Antichrist—the adversary of Christ—will gain worldwide power and unleash terrible persecution against Christians. In the end, Christ will return to earth, destroy the Antichrist, and set up His kingdom forever.

▸ **Chapters 21–22** *The Coming of Eternity*

A new heaven and earth will descend from heaven because the present earth has been destroyed. Within this new heaven and earth resides the new Jerusalem, where there will be no more sin, no more death, and no more suffering. God then ushers in an eternal kingdom marked by righteousness, peace, and love. It is this future kingdom all Christians look forward to with hopeful anticipation.

Putting Meat on the Bones

The word "Revelation" (1:1) means "to uncover or to reveal." God has been in the process of revealing Himself to mankind from the very first verse of the Bible in Genesis. Beginning with His first act of creation, God has been unfolding His eternal destiny for man. With each successive generation He has been guiding the human race toward His ultimate purpose of redeeming His lost creation. Along the way and throughout time, man has resisted God's overtures of redemption. Man has rebelled and suffered the consequences. But there has always been a remnant of people who have desired to know and follow God. Their path of godly living has not been easy. They have been persecuted and killed for their godly passion. But now the book of Revelation shows that the climax is coming. God's promise of the coming King is about to happen. Jesus, the Suffering Servant, the ultimate revelation of God, is returning in all His glory and power to conquer all who have and would defy Him and to rescue His chosen people. History will be complete. Time will cease, and all creation will again be enveloped into eternity.

Fleshing It Out in Your Life

This book is truly "The Revelation of Jesus Christ" (1:1). From the beginning to the end of this glorious book Christ's glory, wisdom, and power are described. The predictions within this book are more relevant today than at any other time in history. As history unfolds itself on a daily basis, the mysteries of this book are beginning to be revealed through modern political and economic policies and military interventions. The beginning signs that the King is coming in judgment are unfolding. For any believer who is compromising with the world, this book is a challenge to refocus on Jesus and His will. For any who have become complacent in zeal for the Lord's return, this book should serve as motivation to a higher level of diligence while watching and waiting for the Lord. Do you believe in His return? And are you prepared for it?

Life Lessons from Revelation

- God controls all people and events—what He says will happen in the future will happen indeed. This should give you confidence for the future.
- In the end, justice and righteousness will prevail. Sin will not continue forever. This should give you encouragement for each and every day of your life.
- Christians will one day become free from this sin-filled world and know perfection and glory in heaven. This should give you hope for eternity.
- God is worthy of worship at all times. This should give you reason to praise Him...now!

Where to Find It

The seven seal judgments 5:1–8:1
The seven trumpet judgments 8:2–11:19
The seven bowl judgments 15:1–16:21
The battle of Armageddon 19:17-19
The casting of Satan into the lake of fire 20:10

Jesus' Comments to the Seven Churches

(2–3)

Church #1: The loveless church—Ephesus
"You have lost your first love" (see 2:4)

Church #2: The persecuted church—Smyrna
"I know how much you have suffered" (2:9)

Church #3: The lax church—Pergamos
"You tolerate sin" (2:14-15)

Church #4: The compromising church—Thyatira
"You permit the teaching of immoral practices" (2:20)

Church #5: The lifeless church—Sardis
"You are dead" (3:1)

Church #6: The obedient church—Philadelphia
"You have...kept My word, and have not denied My name" (3:8)

Church #7: The lukewarm church—Laodicea
"You are neither cold nor hot" (3:15)

The Seven Churches in Revelation 2–3

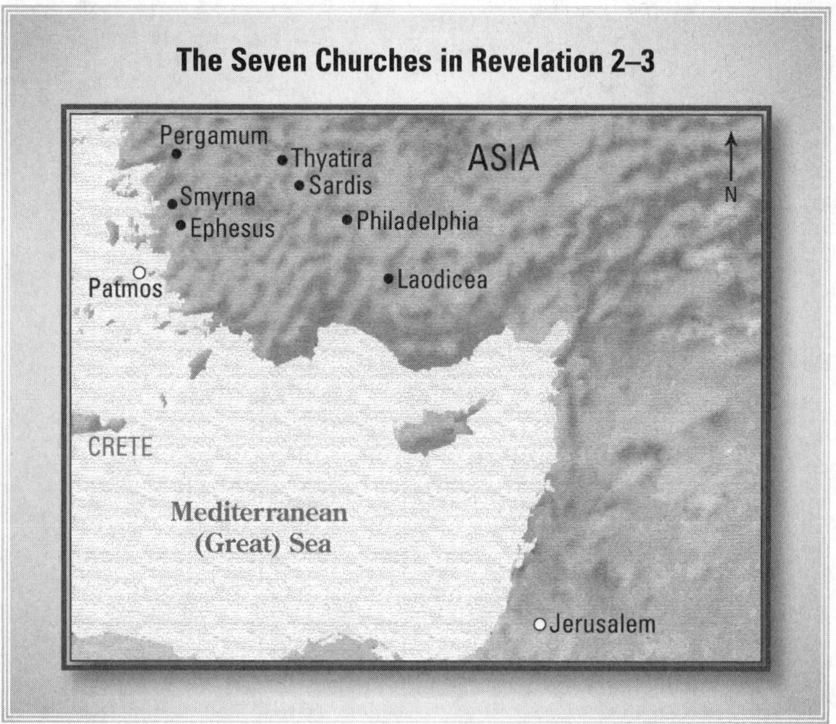

A Final Word

As you finish this book and your journey down the corridors of time, you should now have a better understanding of the full account of God's work in history. Hopefully you have also made many applications of God's truth and have developed a greater appreciation for the relationship He extends to you through His Son, Jesus Christ. Faithful obedience to God's Word is life-changing and results in a closer walk with God.

Before you close the covers of this book, purpose to act on these final steps:

- Purpose to open your heart to the Person of Jesus Christ and the salvation and forgiveness of sin which God extends to you through Him, if you have not already done so—"for there is no other name under heaven given among men by which we must be saved" (Acts 4:12).
- Purpose to continue to "grow in the grace and knowledge of our Lord and Savior Jesus Christ" (2 Peter 3:18).
- Purpose to share God's message of love and redemption with others—the truth that "God so loved the world that He gave His only begotten Son, that whoever believes in Him should not perish but have everlasting life" (John 3:16).

Bare Essentials for Using Your Bible

Themes of All the Books of the Bible

The Old Testament

Genesis . . . . Beginnings
Exodus . . . . Deliverance
Leviticus . . . . Instruction
Numbers . . . . Journeys
Deuteronomy . . . . Obedience
Joshua . . . . Conquest
Judges . . . . Deterioration and deliverance
Ruth . . . . Redemption
1 Samuel . . . . Transition
2 Samuel . . . . Unification
1 Kings. Disruption
2 Kings . . . . Dispersion
1 Chronicles. . . . . Israel's spiritual history
2 Chronicles. . . . . Israel's spiritual heritage
Ezra . . . . Restoration
Nehemiah . . . . Reconstruction
Esther . . . . Preservation
Job . . . . Blessings through suffering
Psalms. . . . . Praise
Proverbs . . . . Practical wisdom
Ecclesiastes. . . . . All is vanity apart from God
Song of Solomon . . . . Love and marriage
Isaiah . . . . Salvation
Jeremiah . . . . Judgment
Lamentations . . . . Lament
Ezekiel. . . . . The glory of the Lord
Daniel . . . . The sovereignty of God
Hosea . . . . Unfaithfulness
Joel. . . . . The day of the Lord

Amos . . . . Judgment
Obadiah . . . . Righteous judgment
Jonah . . . . God's grace to all people
Micah . . . . Divine judgment
Nahum . . . . Consolation
Habakkuk . . . . Trusting a sovereign God
Zephaniah . . . . The "great day of the LORD"
Haggai . . . . Rebuilding the temple
Zechariah . . . . God's deliverance
Malachi . . . . Formalism rebuked

The New Testament

Matthew . . . . The kingdom of God
Mark . . . . The Suffering Servant
Luke . . . . The Perfect Man
John . . . . The Son of God
Acts . . . . The spread of the gospel
Romans . . . . The righteousness of God
1 Corinthians . . . . Christian conduct
2 Corinthians . . . . Paul's defense of his apostleship
Galatians . . . . Freedom in Christ
Ephesians . . . . Blessings in Christ
Philippians . . . . The joy-filled life
Colossians . . . . The supremacy of Christ
1 Thessalonians . . . . Concern for the church
2 Thessalonians . . . . Living in hope
1 Timothy . . . . Instructions for a young disciple
2 Timothy . . . . A charge to faithful ministry
Titus . . . . A manual of conduct
Philemon . . . . Forgiveness
Hebrews . . . . The superiority of Christ
James . . . . Genuine faith
1 Peter . . . . Responding to suffering
2 Peter . . . . Warning against false teachers
1 John . . . . Fellowship with God
2 John . . . . Christian discernment
3 John . . . . Christian hospitality
Jude . . . . Contending for the faith
Revelation . . . . The unveiling of Jesus Christ

How to Study the Bible —Some Practical Tips

One of the noblest pursuits a child of God can embark upon is to get to know and understand God better. The best way we can accomplish this is to look carefully at the book God has written, the Bible, which communicates who He is and His plan for mankind. There are a number of ways we can study the Bible, but one of the most effective and simple approaches to reading and understanding God's Word involves three simple steps:

Step 1: Observation—*What does the passage say?*
Step 2: Interpretation—*What does the passage mean?*
Step 3: Application—*What am I going to do about what the passage says and means?*

Observation

Observation is the first and most important step in the process. As you read the Bible text, you need to look carefully at what is said, and how it is said. Look for:

- *Terms, not words.* Words can have many meanings, but terms are words used in a specific way in a specific context. (For instance, the word *trunk* could apply to a tree, a car, or a storage box. However, when you read, "That tree has a very large trunk," you know exactly what the word means, which makes it a term.)
- *Structure.* If you look at your Bible, you will see that the text has

units called *paragraphs* (indented or marked ¶). A paragraph is a complete unit of thought. You can discover the content of the author's message by noting and understanding each paragraph unit.

- *Emphasis.* The amount of space or the number of chapters or verses devoted to a specific topic will reveal the importance of that topic. (For example, note the emphasis of Romans 9–11 and Psalm 119.)
- *Repetition.* This is another way an author demonstrates that something is important. One reading of 1 Corinthians 13, where the author uses the word "love" nine times in only 13 verses, communicates to us that love is the focal point of these 13 verses.
- *Relationships between ideas.* Pay close attention, for example, to certain relationships that appear in the text:

  —Cause-and-effect: "Well done, good and faithful servant; you were faithful over a few things, I will make you ruler over many things" (Matthew 25:21).

  —Ifs and thens: "If My people who are called by My name will humble themselves, and pray and seek My face, and turn from their wicked ways, then I will hear from heaven and forgive their sin and heal their land" (2 Chronicles 7:14).

  —Questions and answers: "Who is the King of glory? The Lord strong and mighty" (Psalm 24:8).

  Comparisons and contrasts. For example, "You have heard that it was said...but I say to you..." (Matthew 5:21).
- *Literary form.* The Bible is literature, and the three main types of literature in the Bible are discourse (the epistles), prose (Old Testament history), and poetry (the Psalms). Considering the type of literature makes a great deal of difference when you read and interpret the Scriptures.
- *Atmosphere.* The author had a particular reason or burden for writing each passage, chapter, and book. Be sure you notice the mood or tone or urgency of the writing.

After you have considered these things, you then are ready to ask the "Wh" questions:

Who? Who are the people in this passage?
What? What is happening in this passage?

Where?	Where is this story taking place?
When?	What time (of day, of the year, in history) is it?

Asking these four "Wh" questions can help you notice terms and identify atmosphere. The answers will also enable you to use your imagination to re-create the scene you're reading about.

As you answer the "Wh" questions and imagine the event, you'll probably come up with some questions of your own. Asking those additional questions for understanding will help to build a bridge between observation (the first step) and interpretation (the second step) of the Bible study process.

Interpretation

Interpretation is discovering the meaning of a passage, the author's main thought or idea. Answering the questions that arise during observation will help you in the process of interpretation. Five clues (called "the five C's") can help you determine the author's main point(s):

- *Context.* You can answer 75 percent of your questions about a passage when you read the text. Reading the text involves looking at the near context (the verse immediately before and after) as well as the far context (the paragraph or the chapter that precedes and/or follows the passage you are studying).
- *Cross-references.* Let scripture interpret scripture. That is, let other passages in the Bible shed light on the passage you are looking at. At the same time, be careful not to assume that the same word or phrase in two different passages means the same thing.
- *Culture.* The Bible was written long ago, so when we interpret it, we need to understand it from the writers' cultural context.
- *Conclusion.* Having answered your questions for understanding by means of context, cross-reference, and culture, you can make a preliminary statement of the passage's meaning. Remember that if your passage consists of more than one paragraph, the author may be presenting more than one thought or idea.
- *Consultation.* Reading books known as commentaries, which are written by Bible scholars, can help you interpret Scripture.

Application

Application is why we study the Bible. We want our lives to change. We want to be obedient to God and to grow more like Jesus Christ. After we have observed a passage and interpreted or understood it to the best of our ability, we must then apply its truth to our own life.

You'll want to ask the following questions of every passage of Scripture you study:

- How does the truth revealed here affect my relationship with God?
- How does this truth affect my relationship with others?
- How does this truth affect me?
- How does this truth affect my response to the enemy Satan?

The application step is not completed by simply answering these questions. The key is *putting into practice* what God has taught you in your study. Although at any given moment you cannot be consciously applying *every*thing you're learning in Bible study, you can be consciously applying *some*thing. And when you work on applying a truth to your life, God will bless your efforts by, as noted earlier, conforming you to the image of Jesus Christ.

Helpful Bible Study Resources

Concordance—Young's or Strong's
Bible dictionary—Unger's or Holman's
Webster's dictionary
The Zondervan Pictorial Encyclopedia of the Bible
Manners and Customs of the Bible, James M. Freeman

Leading a Bible Study Discussion Group

It is a privilege to lead a Bible study. And what joy and excitement await you as you delve into the Word of God and help others to discover its life-changing truths. If God has called you to lead a Bible study group, I know you'll be spending much time in prayer and planning and giving much thought to being an effective leader. I also know that taking the time to read through the following tips will help you to navigate the challenges of leading a Bible study discussion group and enjoying the effort and opportunity.

The Leader's Roles

As a Bible study group leader, you'll find your role changing back and forth from expert to cheerleader to lover to referee during the course of a session.

Since you're the leader, group members will look to you to be the expert guiding them through the material. So be well prepared. In fact, be over-prepared so that you know the material better than any group member does. Start your study early in the week and let its message simmer all week long. (You might even work several lessons ahead so that you have in mind the big picture and the overall direction of the study.) Be ready to share some additional gems that your group members wouldn't have discovered on their own. That extra insight from your study time—or that comment from a wise Bible teacher or scholar, that clever saying, that keen observation from another believer, and even an appropriate joke—adds an element of fun and keeps Bible study from becoming routine, monotonous, and dry.

Second, be ready to be the group's cheerleader. Your energy and enthusiasm for the task at hand can be contagious. It can also stimulate people to get more involved in their personal study as well as in the group discussion.

Third, be the lover, the one who shows a genuine concern for the members of the group. You're the one who will establish the atmosphere of the group. If you laugh and have fun, the group members will laugh and have fun. If you hug, they will hug. If you care, they will care. If you share, they will share. If you love, they will love. So pray every day to love the people God has placed in your group. Ask Him to show you how to love them with His love.

Finally, as the leader, you'll need to be the referee on occasion. That means making sure everyone has an equal opportunity to speak. That's easier to do when you operate under the assumption that every member of the group has something worthwhile to contribute. So, trusting that the Lord has taught each person during the week, act on that assumption.

Expert, cheerleader, lover, and referee—these four roles of the leader may make the task seem overwhelming. But that's not bad if it keeps you on your knees praying for your group.

A Good Start

Beginning on time, greeting people warmly, and opening in prayer gets the study off to a good start. Know what you want to have happen during your time together and make sure those things get done. That kind of order means comfort for those involved.

Establish a format and let the group members know what that format is. People appreciate being in a Bible study that focuses on the Bible. So keep the discussion on the topic and move the group through the questions. Tangents are often hard to avoid—and even harder to rein in. So be sure to focus on the answers to questions about the specific passage at hand. After all, the purpose of the group is Bible study!

Finally, as someone has accurately observed, "Personal growth is one of the by-products of any effective small group. This growth is achieved when people are recognized and accepted by others. The more friendliness, mutual trust, respect, and warmth exhibited, the more likely that the member will find pleasure in the group, and, too, the more likely the member will work hard toward the accomplishment of the group's goals. The effective leader will strive to reinforce desirable traits" (source unknown).

A Dozen Helpful Tips

Here is a list of helpful suggestions for leading a Bible study discussion group:

1. Arrive early, ready to focus fully on others and give of yourself. If you have to do any last-minute preparation, review, re-grouping, or praying, do it in the car. Don't dash in, breathless, harried, late, still tweaking your plans.
2. Check out your meeting place in advance. Do you have everything you need—tables, enough chairs, a blackboard, hymnals if you plan to sing, coffee, etc.?
3. Greet people warmly by name as they arrive. After all, you've been praying for these people all week long, so let each VIP know that you're glad they've arrived.
4. Use name tags for at least the first two or three weeks.
5. Start on time no matter what—even if only one person is there!
6. Develop a pleasant but firm opening statement. You might say, "This lesson was great! Let's get started so we can enjoy all of it!" or "Let's pray before we begin our lesson."
7. Read the questions, but don't hesitate to reword them on occasion. Rather than reading an entire paragraph of instructions, for instance, you might say, "Question 1 asks us to list some ways that Christ displayed humility. Lisa, please share one way Christ displayed humility."
8. Summarize or paraphrase the answers given. Doing so will keep the discussion focused on the topic, eliminate digressions, help avoid or clear up any misunderstandings of the text, and keep each group member aware of what the others are saying.
9. Keep moving and don't add any of your own questions to the discussion time. It's important to get through the study guide questions.

So if a cut-and-dried answer is called for, you don't need to comment with anything other than a "thank you." But when the question asks for an opinion or an application (for instance, "How can this truth help us in our marriages?" or "How do you find time for your quiet time?"), let all who want to contribute.

10. Affirm each person who contributes, especially if the contribution was very personal, painful to share, or a quiet person's rare statement. Make everyone who shares a hero by saying something like "Thank you for sharing that insight from your own life" or "We certainly appreciate what God has taught you. Thank you for letting us in on it."
11. Watch your watch, put a clock right in front of you, or consider using a timer. Pace the discussion so that you meet your cut-off time, especially if you want time to pray. Stop at the designated time even if you haven't finished the lesson. Remember that everyone has worked through the study once; you are simply going over it again.
12. End on time. You can only make friends with your group members by ending on time or even a little early! Besides, members of your group have the next item on their agenda to attend to—so let them out on time!

Five Common Problems

In any group, you can anticipate certain problems. Here are some common ones that can arise, along with helpful solutions:

1. *The incomplete lesson*—Right from the start, establish the policy that if someone has not done the lesson, it is best for them not to answer the questions. But do try to include their responses to questions that ask for opinions or experiences. Everyone can share some thoughts in reply to a question like, "Reflect on what you know about both athletic and spiritual training and then share what you consider to be the essential elements of training oneself in godliness."
2. *The gossip*—The Bible clearly states that gossiping is wrong, so you don't want to allow it in your group. Set a high and strict standard by saying, "I am not comfortable with this conversation," or "We [not you] are gossiping. Let's move on."

3. *The talkative member*—Here are three scenarios and some possible solutions for each.
   a. Problem talkers may be talking because they have done the homework and are excited about something they have to share. They may also know more about the subject than the others and, if you cut them off, the rest of the group may suffer.
   Solution: Respond with a comment like: "Sarah, you are making very valuable contributions. Let's see if we can get some reactions from the others," or "I know Mike can answer this. He's really done his homework. How about some of the rest of you?"
   b. Talkative members may be talking because they haven't done their homework and want to contribute, but have no boundaries.
   Solution: Establish at the first meeting that those who have not done the lesson do not contribute except on opinion or application questions. You may need to repeat this guideline at the beginning of each session.
   c. Talkative members may want to be heard whether or not they have anything worthwhile to contribute.
   Solution: After subtle reminders, be more direct, saying, "Betty, I know you would like to share your ideas, but let's give others a chance. I'll call on you later."
4. *The quiet member*—Here are two scenarios and possible solutions.
   a. The quiet member wants the floor but somehow can't get the chance to share.
   Solution: Clear the path for the quiet members by first watching for clues that they want to speak (moving to the edge of her seat, looking as if they want to speak, perhaps even starting to say something) and then saying, "Just a second. I think Chris wants to say something." Then, of course, make Chris a hero!
   b. The quiet member simply doesn't want the floor.
   Solution: "Chris, what answer do you have on question 2?" or "Chris, what do you think about...?" Usually after shy people have contributed a few times, they will become more confident and more ready to share. Your role is to provide an opportunity where there is no risk of a wrong answer. But occasionally group members will tell you that they would rather not be called on. Honor the request, but from time to time ask them privately if they feel ready to contribute to the group discussions.

In fact, give all your group members the right to pass. During your first meeting, explain that any time group members do not care to share an answer, they may simply say, "I pass." You'll want to repeat this policy at the beginning of every group session.

5. *The wrong answer*—Never tell group members that they have given a wrong answer, but at the same time never let a wrong answer go by. **Solution:** Either ask if someone else has a different answer or ask additional questions that will cause the right answer to emerge. As the people get closer to the right answer, say, "We're getting warmer! Keep thinking! We're almost there!"

Learning from Experience

Immediately after each Bible study session, evaluate the group discussion time using this checklist. You may also want a member of your group (or an assistant or trainee or outside observer) to evaluate you periodically.

May God strengthen—and encourage—you as you assist others in the discovery of His many wonderful truths.

A One-Year
Daily Bible Reading Plan

January

	Genesis
❑ 1	1–3
❑ 2	4–7
❑ 3	8–11
❑ 4	12–15
❑ 5	16–18
❑ 6	19–22
❑ 7	23–27
❑ 8	28–30
❑ 9	31–34
❑ 10	35–38
❑ 11	39–41
❑ 12	42–44
❑ 13	45–47
❑ 14	48–50
	Exodus
❑ 15	1–4
❑ 16	5–7
❑ 17	8–11
❑ 18	12–14
❑ 19	15–18
❑ 20	19–21
❑ 21	22–24
❑ 22	25–28
❑ 23	29–31
❑ 24	32–34
❑ 25	35–37

- ❑ 26 38–40

Leviticus

- ❑ 27 1–3
- ❑ 28 4–6
- ❑ 29 7–9
- ❑ 30 10–13
- ❑ 31 14–16

February

- ❑ 1 17–20
- ❑ 2 21–23
- ❑ 3 24–27

Numbers

- ❑ 4 1–2
- ❑ 5 3–4
- ❑ 6 5–6
- ❑ 7 7–8
- ❑ 8 9–10
- ❑ 9 11–13
- ❑ 10 14–15
- ❑ 11 16–17
- ❑ 12 18–19
- ❑ 13 20–21
- ❑ 14 22–23
- ❑ 15 24–26
- ❑ 16 27–29
- ❑ 17 30–32
- ❑ 18 33–36

Deuteronomy

- ❑ 19 1–2
- ❑ 20 3–4
- ❑ 21 5–7
- ❑ 22 8–10
- ❑ 23 11–13
- ❑ 24 14–16
- ❑ 25 17–20

❑ 26	21–23
❑ 27	24–26
❑ 28	27–28

March

❑ 1	29–30
❑ 2	31–32
❑ 3	33–34
	Joshua
❑ 4	1–4
❑ 5	5–7
❑ 6	8–10
❑ 7	11–14
❑ 8	15–17
❑ 9	18–21
❑ 10	22–24
	Judges
❑ 11	1–3
❑ 12	4–6
❑ 13	7–9
❑ 14	10–12
❑ 15	13–15
❑ 16	16–18
❑ 17	19–21
	Ruth
❑ 18	1–4
	1 Samuel
❑ 19	1–3
❑ 20	4–6
❑ 21	7–9
❑ 22	10–12
❑ 23	13–14
❑ 24	15–16
❑ 25	17–18
❑ 26	19–20

❑ 27	21–23
❑ 28	24–26
❑ 29	27–29
❑ 30	30–31
	2 Samuel
❑ 31	1–3

April

❑ 1	4–6
❑ 2	7–10
❑ 3	11–13
❑ 4	14–15
❑ 5	16–17
❑ 6	18–20
❑ 7	21–22
❑ 8	23–24
	1 Kings
❑ 9	1–2
❑ 10	3–5
❑ 11	6–7
❑ 12	8–9
❑ 13	10–12
❑ 14	13–15
❑ 15	16–18
❑ 16	19–20
❑ 17	21–22
	2 Kings
❑ 18	1–3
❑ 19	4–6
❑ 20	7–8
❑ 21	9–11
❑ 22	12–14
❑ 23	15–17
❑ 24	18–19
❑ 25	20–22
❑ 26	23–25

1 Chronicles

- ❑ 27 1–2
- ❑ 28 3–5
- ❑ 29 6–7
- ❑ 30 8–10

May

- ❑ 1 11–13
- ❑ 2 14–16
- ❑ 3 17–19
- ❑ 4 20–22
- ❑ 5 23–25
- ❑ 6 26–27
- ❑ 7 28–29

2 Chronicles

- ❑ 8 1–4
- ❑ 9 5–7
- ❑ 10 8–10
- ❑ 11 11–14
- ❑ 12 15–18
- ❑ 13 19–21
- ❑ 14 22–25
- ❑ 15 26–28
- ❑ 16 29–31
- ❑ 17 32–33
- ❑ 18 34–36

Ezra

- ❑ 19 1–4
- ❑ 20 5–7
- ❑ 21 8–10

Nehemiah

- ❑ 22 1–3
- ❑ 23 4–7
- ❑ 24 8–10
- ❑ 25 11–13

Esther

- ❑ 26 1–3
- ❑ 27 4–7
- ❑ 28 8–10

Job

- ❑ 29 1–4
- ❑ 30 5–8
- ❑ 31 9–12

June

- ❑ 1 13–16
- ❑ 2 17–20
- ❑ 3 21–24
- ❑ 4 25–30
- ❑ 5 31–34
- ❑ 6 35–38
- ❑ 7 39–42

Psalms

- ❑ 8 1–8
- ❑ 9 9–17
- ❑ 10 18–21
- ❑ 11 22–28
- ❑ 12 29–34
- ❑ 13 35–39
- ❑ 14 40–44
- ❑ 15 45–50
- ❑ 16 51–56
- ❑ 17 57–63
- ❑ 18 64–69
- ❑ 19 70–74
- ❑ 20 75–78
- ❑ 21 79–85
- ❑ 22 86–90
- ❑ 23 91–98
- ❑ 24 99–104
- ❑ 25 105–107
- ❑ 26 108–113
- ❑ 27 114–118

❑ 28	119
❑ 29	120–134
❑ 30	135–142

July

❑ 1	143–150
	Proverbs
❑ 2	1–3
❑ 3	4–7
❑ 4	8–11
❑ 5	12–15
❑ 6	16–18
❑ 7	19–21
❑ 8	22–24
❑ 9	25–28
❑ 10	29–31
	Ecclesiastes
❑ 11	1–4
❑ 12	5–8
❑ 13	9–12
	Song of Solomon
❑ 14	1–4
❑ 15	5–8
	Isaiah
❑ 16	1–4
❑ 17	5–8
❑ 18	9–12
❑ 19	13–15
❑ 20	16–20
❑ 21	21–24
❑ 22	25–28
❑ 23	29–32
❑ 24	33–36
❑ 25	37–40
❑ 26	41–43

❑ 27	44–46
❑ 28	47–49
❑ 29	50–52
❑ 30	53–56
❑ 31	57–60

August

❑ 1	61–63
❑ 2	64–66
	Jeremiah
❑ 3	1–3
❑ 4	4–6
❑ 5	7–9
❑ 6	10–12
❑ 7	13–15
❑ 8	16–19
❑ 9	20–22
❑ 10	23–25
❑ 11	26–29
❑ 12	30–31
❑ 13	32–34
❑ 14	35–37
❑ 15	38–40
❑ 16	41–44
❑ 17	45–48
❑ 18	49–50
❑ 19	51–52
	Lamentations
❑ 20	1–2
❑ 21	3–5
	Ezekiel
❑ 22	1–4
❑ 23	5–8
❑ 24	9–12
❑ 25	13–15
❑ 26	16–17

- ❑ 27 18–20
- ❑ 28 21–23
- ❑ 29 24–26
- ❑ 30 27–29
- ❑ 31 30–31

September

- ❑ 1 32–33
- ❑ 2 34–36
- ❑ 3 37–39
- ❑ 4 40–42
- ❑ 5 43–45
- ❑ 6 46–48

Daniel

- ❑ 7 1–2
- ❑ 8 3–4
- ❑ 9 5–6
- ❑ 10 7–9
- ❑ 11 10–12

Hosea

- ❑ 12 1–4
- ❑ 13 5–9
- ❑ 14 10–14

- ❑ 15 **Joel**

Amos

- ❑ 16 1–4
- ❑ 17 5–9

- ❑ 18 **Obadiah** and **Jonah**

Micah

- ❑ 19 1–4
- ❑ 20 5–7

- ❑ 21 **Nahum**

❑ 22 **Habakkuk**

❑ 23 **Zephaniah**

❑ 24 **Haggai**

Zechariah

❑ 25 1–4
❑ 26 5–9
❑ 27 10–14

❑ 28 **Malachi**

Matthew

❑ 29 1–4
❑ 30 5–7

October

❑ 1 8–9
❑ 2 10–11
❑ 3 12–13
❑ 4 14–16
❑ 5 17–18
❑ 6 19–20
❑ 7 21–22
❑ 8 23–24
❑ 9 25–26
❑ 10 27–28

Mark

❑ 11 1–3
❑ 12 4–5
❑ 13 6–7
❑ 14 8–9
❑ 15 10–11
❑ 16 12–13
❑ 17 14
❑ 18 15–16

	Luke
❑ 19	1–2
❑ 20	3–4
❑ 21	5–6
❑ 22	7–8
❑ 23	9–10
❑ 24	11–12
❑ 25	13–14
❑ 26	15–16
❑ 27	17–18
❑ 28	19–20
❑ 29	21–22
❑ 30	23–24

	John
❑ 31	1–3

November

❑ 1	4–5
❑ 2	6–7
❑ 3	8–9
❑ 4	10–11
❑ 5	12–13
❑ 6	14–16
❑ 7	17–19
❑ 8	20–21

	Acts
❑ 9	1–3
❑ 10	4–5
❑ 11	6–7
❑ 12	8–9
❑ 13	10–11
❑ 14	12–13
❑ 15	14–15
❑ 16	16–17
❑ 17	18–19
❑ 18	20–21
❑ 19	22–23
❑ 20	24–26

❑ 21	27–28
	Romans
❑ 22	1–3
❑ 23	4–6
❑ 24	7–9
❑ 25	10–12
❑ 26	13–14
❑ 27	15–16
	1 Corinthians
❑ 28	1–4
❑ 29	5–7
❑ 30	8–10

December

❑ 1	11–13
❑ 2	14–16
	2 Corinthians
❑ 3	1–4
❑ 4	5–9
❑ 5	10–13
	Galatians
❑ 6	1–3
❑ 7	4–6
	Ephesians
❑ 8	1–3
❑ 9	4–6
❑ 10	**Philippians**
❑ 11	**Colossians**
❑ 12	**1 Thessalonians**
❑ 13	**2 Thessalonians**

❑ 14 **1 Timothy**

❑ 15 **2 Timothy**

❑ 16 **Titus** and **Philemon**

Hebrews

❑ 17 1–4
❑ 18 5–8
❑ 19 9–10
❑ 20 11–13

❑ 21 **James**

❑ 22 **1 Peter**

❑ 23 **2 Peter**

❑ 24 **1 John**

❑ 25 **2, 3 John, Jude**

Revelation

❑ 26 1–3
❑ 27 4–8
❑ 28 9–12
❑ 29 13–16
❑ 30 17–19
❑ 31 20–22

Other Books by Jim George

Bare Bones Bible Handbook for Teens

Teens will be amazed at how much the Bible has to say about the things that matter most to them—their happiness, friends and family, home and school, and goals for the future.

Know Your Bible from A to Z

This book brings Bible facts to life through more than 150 carefully selected topics that provide fascinating insights about important historical events, interesting customs and cultural practices, and significant people and places.

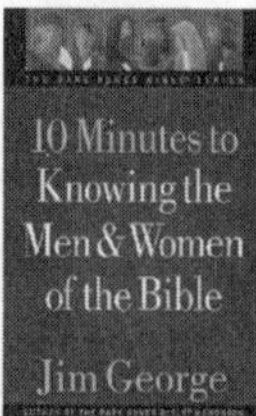

10 Minutes to Knowing the Men and Women of the Bible

The lessons you can learn from the men and women of the Bible are powerfully relevant for today. As you review their lives through the biographical sketches in this book, you'll discover special qualities worth emulating and life lessons for everyday living.

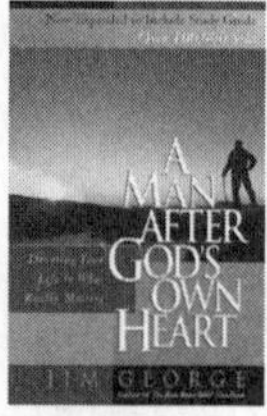

A Man After God's Own Heart

Many Christian men want to be men after God's own heart...but how do they do this? Jim George shows that a heartfelt desire to practice God's priorities is all that's needed. God's grace does the rest. Includes study guide.

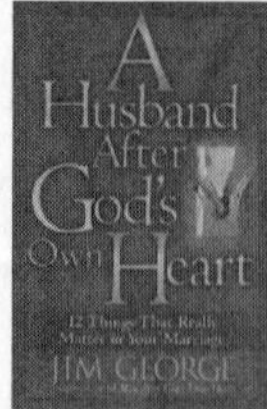

A Husband After God's Own Heart

Husbands will find their marriages growing richer and deeper as they pursue God and discover 12 areas in which they can make a real difference in their relationship with their wife. (This book was a 2005 Gold Medallion Award Finalist.)

A Couple After God's Own Heart
(with Elizabeth George)
Jim and Elizabeth George come together to share from 40-plus years of marital wisdom and experiences to help couples grow closer to each other and to God. You and your spouse will discover how you can enrich your marriage by looking at the lives of key couples in the Bible.

A Boy After God's Own Heart
Jim George helps young guys to understand why God is important in everything they do. He teaches what the Bible says about parents, making right choices, choosing good friends, taking school seriously, and following after God.

A Boy's Guide to Making Really Good Choices
It's never too early to give young boys a resource that will help them learn the skills for making right choices in life. *A Boy's Guide to Making Really Good Choices* is designed to help boys ages 8-12 learn how to think through their options, realize the possible consequences, and develop good decision-making skills.

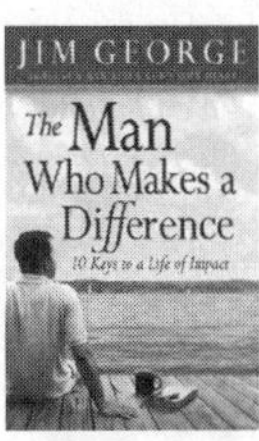

The Man Who Makes a Difference
What made the apostle Paul so effective, so influential? Readers will experience true fulfillment as they learn how they can make a real and lasting difference in the workplace, at home, at church, and in their community.

The Remarkable Prayers of the Bible
Jim looks deeply into prayers of great men and women in the Bible and shares more than a hundred practical applications that can help shape our own lives and prayers. A separate *Growth and Study Guide* is also available.

A Young Man After God's Own Heart
Pursuing God really *is* an adventure—a lot like climbing a mountain. There are all kinds of challenges on the way up, but the awesome view at the top is well worth the trip. This book helps teen men to experience the thrill of knowing real success in life—the kind that counts with God. (This book was a 2006 Gold Medallion Award Finalist.)

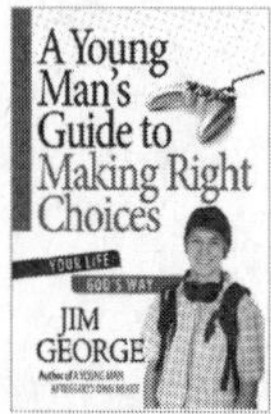

A Young Man's Guide to Making Right Choices
This book will help teen men to think carefully about their decisions, assuring a more fulfilling and successful life. A great resource for gaining the skills needed to face life's challenges.

God Loves His Precious Children
(*coauthored with Elizabeth George*)
Jim and Elizabeth George share the comfort and assurance of Psalm 23 with young children. Engaging watercolor scenes and delightful rhymes bring the truths and promises of each verse to life.

God's Wisdom for Little Boys
(*coauthored with Elizabeth George*)
The wonderful teachings of Proverbs come to life for boys. Memorable rhymes play alongside colorful paintings for an exciting presentation of truths to live by.

A Little Boy After God's Own Heart
(*coauthored with Elizabeth George*)
With delightful artwork by Judy Luenebrink, this book encourages young boys in the virtues of patience, goodness, faithfulness, sharing, and more. Written to help boys discover how special they are, these rhymes present wisdom and character traits for life.

An Invitation to Write

Jim George is a teacher and speaker and the author of several books, including *A Man After God's Own Heart.* If you would like to receive more information about other books and audio products by Jim George, to sign up for his mailings, or to share how *The Bare Bones Bible® Handbook* has influenced your life, you can write to Jim at:

Jim and Elizabeth George Ministries
P.O. Box 2879
Belfair, WA 98528
www.JimGeorge.com